no, you can't

no, you can't

aim low and give up winning for good

dave dunseath

HarperCollins
Leadership

AN IMPRINT OF HarperCollins

Published by HarperCollins Leadership, an imprint of HarperCollins Focus LLC.

Any internet addresses, phone numbers, or company or product information printed in this book are offered as a resource and are not intended in any way to be or to imply an endorsement by HarperCollins, nor does HarperCollins vouch for the existence, content, or services of these sites, phone numbers, companies, or products beyond the life of this book.

ISBN 978-1-4041-1004-5 (SC)
ISBN 978-1-4041-1005-2 (eBook)

Printed in the United States of America
20 21 22 23 24 LSC 6 5 4 3 2 1

TO MY PARENTS,

for always smiling and nodding
every time I told them my writing
career was going well

If at first you don't
succeed, try, try, again. Then quit.
There's no use in being
a damn fool about it.

—W. C. FIELDS

contents

acknowledgments

A million and one thank-you's should be divided equally amongst the following people who deemed my scribblings worthy of real estate in a bookstore: Bryan Curtis, Pamela Clements, Jennifer Greenstein, Laura Troup, Ashley Earnhardt-Aiken, Stacy Clark, Damon Reiss, Ty Powers, and Stephanie Newton.

Last, but certainly not least, my heartfelt thanks to June Johnson, Pamela Clements's mom, without whom this book may never have seen the light of day. Through her laughter, a dream came true for me.

introduction

I was going to buy a copy of *The Power of Positive Thinking*, and then I thought: What the hell good would that do?

—RONNIE SHAKES

I hate book intros. It's like waiting in line for the amusement park to open. Why the park was built and who inspired it are of no interest to me when I'm fixated on the giant roller coaster just beyond the gate. Besides, if a book is well written, I don't think it needs an intro.

So I wrote an intro. I wrote it because it's the law. It's an unwritten law—but it is the law nonetheless. Like having to wait in long lines at the amusement park. So if you're already bored, feel free to hop the gate and make a mad dash for the coaster.

In the meantime, how about a quick game of "What If?" What if I handed you a book right now called *Walking on Your Hands Is Fun*—would you want to read it? What if you found a book at a yard sale called *Hand Walking for Dummies*—would you buy it? What if I gave you tickets to a two-day seminar called "Standing on Your Own Two Hands"—would you go?

No—you wouldn't. You wouldn't because learning how to walk on your hands is ridiculous. It's unnatural. Try it and in five seconds you'd be playing a different game called "What's the Point?" Simply put, walking on your hands is a behavior contrary to your normal state of being.

Yet how many of today's bestselling books attempt to change you or inspire you to think, act, or do things contrary to your normal behavior? They are the teachings of shameless profiteers preaching the gospels of discipline, motivation, and achieving goals. All that really means is these authors will gladly share with you—for a profit—their alleged formulas for success. *Success* is just a fancy word for winning. And winning, for most of us, is about as natural as walking around on our hands.

The message, of course, is that winning is good and losing is bad. The authors of these books want us to believe that anyone can be a winner. Meanwhile, those of us working for companies that buy into this propaganda are sent away to be brainwashed and mentally tortured in sunless chambers called *motivational seminars.*

If losing is actually something everybody does normally—that is to say, if more people tend to finish between second and last place—then it seems to me we should be celebrating entire lives spent in vain, torment, and frustration. It is our nature to lose. For rarely, if ever, are we winners.

So, are you a loser? What does it mean if you are?

It means you were invited to life's big banquet and ended

up working the drive-thru. It means you've been filling your head with lies, starting your days with sayings such as "You're a winner!" or "Yes, you can!" when you know you can't or you would have by now. I've found the later you get up in the day, the less often you'll lie to yourself about how unique and brilliant and successful you're going to be.

Loser implies many things. But all it really means is that you're good at doing just one thing—not winning.

Let me say that again: being a loser doesn't necessarily mean you're a failure. It just means you're not a winner. And because you do *not* win a heck of a lot more than you *do* win, it stands to reason that you're either on the verge of losing or you're already busy taking orders at the drive-thru. By the way, working the drive-thru does not make you a loser. Pretending the new guy on fries is below you does.

Now, once in a great while, despite your efforts, you will win. You will. It's the law of averages, and that's one law a loser knows a thing or two about. Though on those rare occasions when you do win, it's likely your victory had more to do with everyone else not winning. Remember, winning is always the exception. It can't last and it won't last. Winning cannot be repeated at will. It is not a habit. Losing is a habit because losing fits the three characteristics that define what a habit is: you do it all the time, you do it without thinking about it, and you know you're going to do it even before you do it.

Losing is truly the one thing we rarely fail at succeeding in. In fact, in any competition, if you didn't finish first, guess what—you didn't finish second. You lost, my friend.

Question: What is the difference between second and last place?

Answer: Nothing.

What is second place? Second place is merely the highest point a loser can reach. And since you've got a pretty good track record of always coming in somewhere other than first, why not start aiming for targets you already know you can hit?

That's what this book is about. You should never be disappointed about coming in second—or fourth or even ninth—if you weren't expecting to come in first anyway.

Coming up short in life is as easy as breathing. You can practically do it without thinking. And all the skills required to get there—like cheating or making excuses or even quitting—take less time to learn than you might imagine. A whole lot less. All you really need is a little bit of effort and a very small amount of know-how. In fact, your expectations can go so low that anything you do achieve is completely surprising. And when you're good, that's always good enough.

But up until now, where could you find great advice like this? There are no books in the library entitled *Losing for Dummies*. Don't bother checking the phone book for a Losers Anonymous meeting. And don't ask anyone at an Amway convention what being a *loser* is—they don't know the meaning of the word.

You know, as far back as I can remember, I was fooled into believing the impossible. When I was four, I believed in Santa Claus. When I was ten, I thought I could jump off the roof and fly. But does knowing the truth about Santa diminish my love of Christmas? Did a separated shoulder inspire me to jump from higher rooftops? Not really. Now my lack of believing and total lack of discipline spare me from inevitable failures and disappointing outcomes.

I can't tell you what a relief it is to know I'll never make a difference. It's the most freeing feeling in the world knowing that whatever I want—whatever I'm chasing—has already been accomplished, already been achieved, or already been proven it can't be done by someone else. Thanks, someone else.

Now, I am a contented underachiever. I am a typical, random, average nonsuccess. I know that having a yes-I-can attitude will not make me the president or an astronaut or

Tiger Woods. That doesn't make me a bad person. I have never been voted off the island. I have never bid more than the actual retail price. But I am a loser. I've got the T-shirt, and I've seen the movie. All I would like to do is share with you how easy and simple an average life can be when you don't waste time reaching for improbable goals, clinging to faded hopes, or holding on to impossible dreams.

That's all a loser is, really. A loser is anyone who almost touched a star, almost held a dream, or almost got his wish. It's anyone who doesn't win and calls it fate or destiny or bad karma or jinxed. Take it from me, once you make your way from *Loserindenialus* to *Loserallthetimeus*, you'll have tons of great excuses to choose from—anytime you need one. All you have to do is let go of what you never were and quit imagining all the things you'll never be.

So don't be afraid to give up believing in what is too difficult, too unlikely, or nearly impossible. Don't be afraid to quit often, make excuses, or expect the worse. Don't be afraid to let your good intentions sit idly by while you cruise through your days underperforming.

I'll warn you now, you're going to find some real winners out there who would love to dismiss these concepts as foolish and ridiculous. I know this goes without saying, but don't listen to them. If you're like me, you haven't taken advice from a winner in a long time.

I'm gonna leave you with four words every loser knows: *nearly, almost, close,* and *if.* These words are the mating calls of losers everywhere. Whistle one and a flock of losers will be whistling back a chorus of *nearly hads, almost mades, oh so closes,* and *if if ifs.*

And you should find the following phrase helpful when your dreams start getting too big. It's the Loser's Creed:

No, I can't,
or I would have by now.

Say it enough, believe it enough, and you'll feel like you've died and gone to Disneyland. You'll be in a place where you're never concerned about hard work, a place where you never feel guilty for goofing off all day, a place where nobody expects anything from you, a place where choosing to eat a third corn dog—or not—will be the hardest decision of your day.

One last thing. Every chapter in this book concludes with a list of Affirmations. Like all affirmations, the more you repeat them, the more they will benefit you. Read them daily—out loud when possible. In fact, take them with you everywhere you go—even keep some in the bathroom. Since bathroom visits are about as close as you get to having any real success these days, why not reward those efforts with a handful of Affirmations?

I can't promise you'll be a loser if you follow and apply all the guidelines I've presented in this book. But you will go as far in this world as you thought you would.

And if you make it all the way to the end without nodding off or wanting your money back, that'll be another bet my publisher just lost.

reality check

Anytime you hear someone say
it's a win-win situation,
they either don't know all the facts
or they have a stuttering problem.

chapter one

history of losers

History is a set of lies agreed upon.

—NAPOLEON BONAPARTE

nce upon a time, long ago and far away, before diet sodas and sacrifice bunts, three ships sailed across the Atlantic and changed the world forever. They were the *Niña*, the *Pinta,* and the *Santa Maria.*

But they were not alone.

Following in their wake were three lesser-known ships. They were the *Blamer,* the *Avoider,* and the *Envier.*

So who were these distant finishers, these forgotten souls whose spirit and vision led them to see the world as Blamers, Avoiders, and Enviers? Well, few apparently knew where they were headed. Most, if not all, believed their journey would never succeed. We do know that as soon as they reached the shore, they stuck an umbrella and an ice chest in the sand and declared it the Beach. They loved the Beach, even though it was crowded with pricey condos and two-hundred-dollar rounds of golf.

They made their way inland but would return every year to the same beach. Everyone talked about how wonderful the Beach was and agreed that anything was better than wearing a tie to work.

The Blamers, Avoiders, and Enviers spent their days waiting for things that never seemed to happen, so they gave up trying. They fought constantly against a ruthless tribe of pillagers called the Creditors. Yet they still managed to fill countless hours of free time playing games. Their favorite game was called the "Complaining Game." The object of the Complaining Game was to figure out why they had to do things they didn't like doing and why they weren't getting to do things other people were getting to do. They played the Complaining Game every chance they could, even though it always ended the same way and everyone went home a loser.

Then one day, three more ships arrived. They were the *Lawyer,* the *Attorney,* and the *Paralegal.* No one could tell them apart, so everyone just referred to them as *My Lawyer.*

The Blamers, the Avoiders, and the Enviers invited My Lawyer over for an evening of Complaining. My Lawyer loved the Complaining Game but suggested three things be included to make the game more enjoyable: billable hours, consultation fees, and outrageous cash settlements. They called their new game "Filing Lawsuits."

My Lawyer told everyone their new game would make them all winners. And as long as they continued Filing Lawsuits with My Lawyer, they could do all the Complaining they wanted, but they could do it back at the Beach from a pricey condo in between two-hundred-dollar rounds of golf—and never have to wear a tie to work again.

And everybody was happy.

So to this day, the descendants of those original Blamers, Avoiders, and Enviers continue to work as hard as their ancestors did. For they, too, believe it really doesn't matter whether you win or lose, as long as you know My Lawyer.

chapter two

ethics

What's the good of a lie if it's seen through?
When I tell a lie, no one can tell it
from the gospel truth.
Sometimes I can't even tell it myself.
—GRAHAM GREENE

Ethics. It's the stuff of good parenting. It teaches kids right from wrong. Vice from virtue. It makes black-and-white of good and evil. As children, we were rewarded for displaying ethical behavior—honesty, fortitude, and self-denial. We were admonished for our unethical actions—lying, cheating, and manipulating others. We were taught early on that there is a difference between a shopping spree and a killing spree. We learned that it is the act or absence of ethics that separates us into good and bad citizens.

Of course, we're adults now, aren't we? We have neither the time nor the freedom to behave like children. We have adult responsibilities, and with those responsibilities come hard decisions that have us doing things we don't necessarily like to do. But we do them. So while children play their little game of "Right and Wrong," we as adults have to play another game called "Truth or Consequences."

Consequences is just a fancy word for results—and unfavorable results are the consequences of going around and telling the truth all day long.

Have you seen the movie *Liar Liar*? It's the story of a

successful lawyer who—through a selfish wish from his own son—receives a curse that forces him to speak the truth for twenty-four hours. His life is quickly reduced to shambles. Why this movie is considered a comedy is beyond me. It is nothing short of horrifying to watch someone have to tell the truth all the time. Honestly, we don't necessarily want to hear the truth any more than we like having to say it. Thankfully, we don't have to very often.

Do you know there are only three people in the world that will always tell you the truth? Only three. They're your mother, your doctor, and your waiter. So when you hear "I love you," "You have six months to live," and "You do get fries with that," you can believe it. The rest of the time you are being lied to and manipulated.

Question is: Is lying ethical or unethical?

Two things should help clear that up for you. First, pretty much everything is a gray area. Second, nothing is ever black-and-white.

Here's a hypothetical question: you walk out of a store with an item you were not charged for. Did you just steal something?

Here is where folks get into trouble. When you're trying to determine the rightness or wrongness of anything, your first question should always be: Are you in any danger of going to prison? That will determine what the rest of your answers should be. Then try asking some questions that will make you feel better about an ethically challenging moment. Was it only a small-dollar item? Was it from a store that's been gouging you for years? Would you only get the clerk fired if you took the item back? As you can see, it's rarely a black-and-white world we live in.

The first rule of ethics:

Find out if a wrong answer could put you in jail. That will determine the right answer.

You know, when I was little I wanted to be what every other kid wanted to be—a circus clown. But I grew up. I traded in my clown suit and stopped pretending I liked other people's kids. And then something else happened on the road from adolescent immaturity to adult immaturity. Survival dumped idealism, slept with the truth, and produced a little bundle of joy called Reality. A short time later Reality got a little brother named Ethics.

Well, it wasn't long before Reality smacked Ethics in the face while Ethics had a choke hold on Reality. They struggled and argued constantly. They went together like Seventh-day Adventists and brewery tours. But after seeing how much money could be made by tolerating each other, Reality and Ethics formed a truce, shared an apartment, and pretended to be friends. As long as they're never in the same room together, they get along just fine.

Let's try another hypothetical situation and see how you're coming along. Would you say that doing a favor in order to receive a favor is manipulation? By the way, the word *manipulation* comes from the French phrase *auvré minute es borne le succour*. If you make a sale based on manipulation, you still get the commission. *Commission* is just a fancy word for money, and money is what it takes to feed your family. Well, the last I heard, feeding your family is hardly unethical. It's quite the opposite. So, if you "manipulate" someone into believing they're making a smart decision for buying more than they need or can afford, that does not make you ethically challenged. What it does make you is twice the commission.

The second rule of ethics:

If you can get somebody to do something without threatening them with their lives, it's not unethical.

Don't get me wrong. Doing the right thing is a great idea. You always want to try for another merit badge to impress the other scouts. But if you really want to get ahead faster in this world, then sometimes a less-than-accurate answer might be to your advantage.

The third rule of ethics:

The right answer is always the answer that closes the deal, makes you twice the money, or gets her to agree to go out with you.

Does this mean there are times when two wrongs can make a right? Well, I think it's safe to assume that people in dangerous situations look for solutions. If you were an astronaut in trouble, that's exactly what you'd do. You'd look for the fastest and easiest way out of your bad situation. You'd want a favorable outcome and would do whatever it took to make it happen, wouldn't you?

Say you're a teenager and your parents catch you with an illicit substance. Like an astronaut in a malfunctioning space capsule, you are in trouble. Well, born losers are not born liars, but who would benefit from the truth at this point? Not you. You already know the truth. Your parents are hoping to hear what you hope is going to sound like the truth. Just as any astronaut would do, you act quickly and decisively. You find the courage to say what has to be said and you tell them, "I was just keeping it for a friend." Your parents are thrilled, and you are saved from certain death. Call me a hopeless romantic, but I don't know how a fairy-tale ending like that could ever be considered wrong.

So, can you really lie, cheat, steal, and manipulate others and still be considered an honest person? Sure you can. We lie all the time to ugly people and tell them they look great or beautiful or whatever. You're giving their self-esteem a huge boost while you're flat-out lying to their faces. That's not unethical. That's not wanting to be alone at 2 a.m. when the bar is closing and you're far from home, which brings us to the fourth rule of ethics.

The fourth rule of ethics:

The only thing more subjective than beauty is unethical behavior.

Answer this: Is getting free cable or using pirate cards to get free satellite TV wrong? First, are you the one getting it? Second, what are the chances of actually getting caught and doing any hard time? Besides, what exactly would you be accused of stealing—electrical impulses and invisible wavelengths? They'd have to start arresting people for stealing oxygen and gravity.

Think of ethics as a valley between where you are and where you want to be. The challenge is to take the easiest path as far as you can until extenuating circumstances compel you to take detours and alternate routes to increase your odds of a favorable outcome. Isn't that how Tom Hanks brought *Apollo 13* safely back to earth?

We are all running around in an invisible world called a "Gray Area." And most of your decisions about how to get around in a Gray Area come from years of being stepped on, stepped over, and taken advantage of. Those who prosper have long since put away their childhood maps and discovered a world of secret passages, detours, and alternative routes.

Losing is not just about quitting at the drop of a hat or giving up before you even try, although that is a good start. Losing is about making a commitment to sacrificing principles—no matter what the cost. It's about turning life's ordinary, everyday challenges into halfhearted efforts. It's about allowing other people's excuses to become your own.

It's believing that ethics is a Gray Area where victories justify the means, the means justify the money, and not telling the truth always falls under the "no harm, no foul" rule.

Bending the rules to get you out of a dangerous situation is not unethical. Using any and all means necessary to get you where you need to go is not unethical. Doing what you have to do to survive is not unethical. How can it be? Astronauts do it all the time.

ethics affirmations

→ Manipulation is my way of capitalizing on the weak-nesses of the less astute.

→ If I'm still black-and-white on issues of ethics, then I must be retired, in the clergy, or just not interested in job advancement.

→ I should always attempt to do what's right, but only if I have the available time and money to do so.

→ Lying isn't wrong if it keeps me from spending the night alone.

→ Two wrongs don't make a right unless it gets me out of serious trouble.

→ If I misbehave and nobody sees me, that's one less lie I'll have to tell later.

→ There are always extenuating circumstances.

→ The first—and most important—rule of ethics is always establishing if a wrong answer could put me in jail. That alone determines the right answer.

reality check

Admit your mistakes and you will mature and grow. Don't admit them and you might get away with it.

chapter three

parenting

Happiness is having a large, loving, caring,
close-knit family in another city.
—GEORGE BURNS

The best things you can give your children are the same things your parents gave you: fear, guilt, and anxiety. These will help kids keep their guard up in an uncertain world.

For parents, fear rules. Fear is like risk prevention for the soul. Fear lets others make decisions so you can remain blameless. Fear prevents embarrassing moments from ever starting by keeping you out of situations where results are unpredictable. Fear keeps you from attempting the impossible.

Fear is the invisible leash that keeps your kids from playing piñata with the neighbor's cat. Ask any parent and they'll tell you it's only the fear of Santa watching that keeps little boys from kicking each other in the jimmies during the holidays. But the moment Christmas is over, there isn't an eight-year-old alive with an older brother who isn't dropping to his knees and humming *The Nutcracker Suite* like a natural-born soprano.

Those are just the ways kids behave when fear is real and when it isn't. That's why it's crucial for you, as the parent, to provide your children with a backup system when fear breaks down and is unable to govern their behavior. Moms call this little miracle "guilt."

Apart from television, guilt is the only thing controlling your kids when you need to take a little break from "parenting." Guilt is what makes your kids feel bad for not doing the things they should be doing, and worse for doing things they enjoy doing.

The fear of failure is one of life's lessons that kids rarely get over. It starts in elementary school as the fear of being ridiculed and carries over into the teen years as the fear of being rejected. Giving your kids the gifts of shame and humiliation early on will make it less traumatic for them once they start getting picked on and beaten up in middle school. And once guilt gets a good foothold, your kids won't do all the things you don't want them doing when you—or fear—cannot step in quickly enough. You'll never again worry whether your children have enough anxiety or fear to control their behavior. Guilt is that good.

Life is simply too unpredictable and uncertain to try to instill consistent habits and routines. That's why telling your little ones that nothing they do is right and never offering any encouragement are the best ways to prepare them for living and working in the real world.

So why are we as parents running to shrinks to try to undo all the bad, evil things our parents did to us when those are the very things we're passing on to our own kids? It's because our parents told us when we were little that if we just believed in ourselves, someday we could be a movie star or a professional athlete or even the president of the United States. If you ask me, it's a bad idea to tell children they can grow up to become anything they want to be. You're only making sure they end up in therapy to overcome inferiority complexes for attempting things they were never capable of achieving. Kids need constant reminding that, even as adults, they will get burned when playing with fire. Despite numerous songs to the contrary, we don't have wings and we cannot fly. The world is a dangerous place. Safety and success are uncertain.

Of course, the very things we failed so horribly in are the very things we want to protect our kids from—risk, uncertainty, and Algebra II. The question now is twofold. How do we protect our kids once they're out from under our wings? And how do we pick them up after their dreams come crashing down around them?

Well, the bad news is they can't be picked up, dusted off, and made to dream even bigger. They're just like you, remember? The good news is you can tweak your child's spirit very early on to help prepare him for failure. By "tweak" I mean numb. Numbing a child's spirit will make it easier to withstand the endless string of crushing defeats that await him in some crappy job his guidance counselor kept referring to as "a promising career."

The same technique you use on your child to protect her from a hostile world can and should be used to prepare yourself for a day at the office. Numb your spirit and you'll find yourself spending less time worrying over things you once wished for. Daydreaming may have carried you through school, but it won't get you out of the mailroom.

Show me someone who is content and satisfied with a 9-to-5 job, and I'll show you a mild-mannered adult who owes his parents a debt of gratitude for raising him in a home filled with constant anxiety, countless fears, and endless guilt. Fear equals job security. It saves you from termination by keeping you from speaking up for yourself in front of superiors. When fear is not enough, you can usually rely on a host of other anxieties to keep you loyal and compliant. The point is, the more fear you give your kids, the longer they'll hang on to a demeaning—yet less challenging—job later in life. Now, what parents wouldn't want that kind of job security for their child?

Think of parenting as a family tradition of fear, anxiety, and guilt being passed down from your parents to your kids. You're a delivery system now for a host of psychoses, anxieties, and nervous disorders. So don't feel bad when you begin sentences with "How stupid are you . . ." or "Only an idiot . . ." Those are words your four-year-old needs to hear sometimes to get the point across. It'll work on him like it worked on you.

And whatever you do, stop trying to appear sane all the

time. That's a weakness for most parents, and if there's one thing a kid likes more than the smell of his own farts is the stench of parental weakness. Kids respond to what they see, and until they see you wearing double-knit slacks, a zipper at half mast, and a lampshade on your head, they know they're not too late to the party.

And speaking of good parenting, there's a lot of gobbledy-gook about how to discipline "today's kids." Allow me to let you in on a little secret. Kids are capable of appearing only one of two ways—cute or demon possessed. When they're demon possessed, give them what they want until their heads stop spinning and the creepy voices disappear. In those rare moments when they're cute, that's when you should take advantage of their adoring love and start loading them up with anxiety, fear, and guilt.

If you only remember one thing from this chapter, I hope it's that when you compete for your children's love by buying gifts and indulging them in unacceptable behavior, you're not only good to skip to the next chapter, you're also guarantee-ing that they'll like you a lot more than the other parent after the divorce. Buying affection is a time-proven method for making sure your kids will love you every other weekend and two full weeks in the summer.

Quitting often in life is acceptable and at times necessary—but not when it comes to parenting. Never stop sharing your love of yelling and screaming at your kids, and never stop giving them the time of day you plan on getting home from the bar. Once they feel certain that your attention span is short, unfocused, and never fully on them, then you won't have to worry anymore if your kids are gonna turn out to be just like you. How could they become anything else?

parenting affirmations

→ All parenting means is that I am passing on a host of anxieties, quirks, and nervous disorders from one generation to the next.

→ Telling my kids that nothing they do is right and never offering encouragement are the best ways to prepare them for jobs in the real world.

→ I'm preparing my kids for life by focusing on their failures. Once they learn to expect the worst, they'll be disappointed less often.

→ Every time I buy my children's love by giving them tons of frivolous gifts, I'm practically guaranteeing that after the divorce I'll be the parent they like the most.

→ Giving my kids the gifts of shame and humiliation early on will make it less traumatic for them once they start getting picked on and beaten up at school.

chapter four

success

The worst part about having success is trying
to find someone who is happy for you.

—BETTE MIDLER

emember all the things you said you were gonna be when you grew up? Are you any of those things now? Chances are you're not. Dreaming big usually leads to failure. I mean, it ain't called dreaming for nothing.

The genius in setting impossible goals is that no one believes you can really reach them. That's why your childhood friends don't raise an eyebrow when you tell them you're not an astronaut or a matador or a professional whatever. Chances are, none of your friends are astronauts or matadors either. That's also why your closest friends belittle, humiliate, and remind you of all the things you aren't or never will be. They're supposed to tell you the truth.

Try telling your best friend you're moving out west to ski all day and DJ all night, and she'll call you crazy. She'll flat out tell you it can't be done. But tell your friend over a bottle of Jack Daniels that you're moving out west to ski all day and DJ all night and she'll make you swear to take her with you. There is nothing in this world that can't be dreamed up over a bottle of Jack and not sound completely believable.

Goals are not reached for two simple reasons: you didn't

believe you could do it and the bank didn't believe it either. Bankers, unfortunately, don't make deals over shots of Jack.

But the biggest reason people struggle to be successful, according to winners, is that their intentions lack clarity. If you have a goal you still believe you can reach, try stating exactly what you're going to do. Don't be vague about it. Don't just say you're going bowling tonight. Say you're going to the bowling alley to drink away years of regret and shame because you've lost all hope of becoming anything more than who and what you are right now. I guarantee if you say it enough times, that's exactly what will happen.

They say there are many roads to success. Well, not yours—but in general, I think they mean it's simply a matter of analyzing what you want out of life and coming up with a plan to reach those goals—unless your psychic says otherwise. Do psychics know more about you than you do? You bet. That's what makes them psychic.

Losers have an uncanny ability to seek and follow advice that is often unreliable and frequently inaccurate. It would explain why losers rarely go to doctors and civil engineers to find out who their true love is. And though psychics have varying degrees of ability regarding insight, they all have extremely keen eyesight. That's why you never have to call ahead for an appointment, because a psychic can see you coming a mile away.

So is there really any difference between failing to reach a goal and succeeding at being a failure? There is if you still see a difference between second and last place.

Every failure should be a learning experience that keeps us from failing over and over again. It should be, but it rarely is. Losing is simply too addictive. It's habit-forming and difficult to stop. In fact, it's easier to quit smoking than to stop losing. That's why patches and hypnosis have very little effect on losers. And willpower? Forget about it. You yourself know you can't just wake up and say, "Today I will not lose." Trust me, anyone who believes in willpower doesn't know the first thing about losing.

Failure usually means just one thing—you're doing everything wrong. You either finish a winner or not a winner. Beyond that it's all self-help books and shrink doctors giving false assurances to those who still think they're not destined for failure. Nowadays, they'll try to convince losers they're winners just for trying. How confusing is that?

We've practically grown up being encouraged to lose. Were you ever told as a child after a crushing defeat that it wasn't about winning or losing, it was about how you played the game? So what is everybody crying about on Oprah? Small successes may slow down your rate of failure, but short of winning, you lost. And a loss does not a winner make.

Success generally comes to those who have three things

going for them: luck, connections, and a six-figure income. But do you want to know the real difference between being successful and being where you are right now? The real difference is what estate attorneys call "an inheritance." Sure, you can dream big and study hard and set goals and work all the hours you want. But think about it, has anyone ever worked really hard and died broke working for a dream they never reached? More have than not, my friend.

If at any point before you retire, you haven't hit the lottery or been able to collect on the untimely, yet fortuitous, death of a spouse, then you better get to praying that you've got a wealthy rancher for an uncle who's about to saddle up for his last roundup and you're his sole beneficiary. Of course, it takes more than just getting an inheritance to come out a winner. You'll need a pot of gold the size of King Kong's cereal bowl if you're hoping for early retirement.

The following are a few truths and myths to help you understand what success is really all about:

Truth: Success is for anyone who has the conviction and the desire to lie, cheat, or do things that might be considered wrong.

Truth: Success is not
a habit. Habits are things
you can't stop doing, like
smoking and losing.

Myth: If you're doing your
very best and you're still
not successful, that doesn't
necessarily mean you're
always going to be a failure.
Wrong. Yeah, it usually does.

Myth: Success and prosperity
go hand in hand. Wrong.
You can successfully eat
everything on your plate
and still owe two months
back rent.

If you really want to succeed at losing all the time, then
you will have to commit to quitting all the time. But people
have the misconception that quitting means giving up.

Wrong. Wrong, wrong, wrong.

The difference between quitting and giving up is that quitting means you'll no longer be wasting other people's time. Giving up means you'll no longer be wasting your time. So the question is, does quitting make you a loser? Well, think of it this way: If you're tired of losing and you quit, wouldn't that stop you from being even more of a loser than you already are?

Quitting is like hitting the exit door early during a bad movie. It's all about developing a sense of knowing when enough is enough. Once you become comfortable with the idea of quitting, you'll usually walk out long before the credits roll. In time, you'll wonder why you've waited so long to quit projects or commitments that were up to 95 percent complete. But don't expect praises for saving you and everybody else 5 percent in wasted time and money. It ain't comin'.

Have you ever heard of someone having what's called a "fear of success"? Well, plenty more have a fear of quitting, but quitting is actually very easy to do. Knowing when to quit is where things get dicey. That's why real losers quit often and quit early. Just try it a few times and see how easy it really is. Who knows, you might take to quitting like a ballplayer to steroids.

One of the first things you can quit doing is believing the lies regarding success. It's a proven fact that taking risks leads to stress. Stress leads to heart attacks and heart attacks lead to dying. Remember that the next time you hear someone say they're dying to be successful. It's a good idea not to attempt things that could kill you just for trying.

The only real change you probably need to make is to be more honest with yourself and with others. You know success isn't about hard work and commitment. It's about holding out for signing bonuses, demanding severance packages, and kicking back and waiting for Father Time to take out some of your wealthier kinfolk.

When someone asks what you would do differently if you could live your life over, tell them next time you'd like to be born with a gold-plated silver spoon in your mouth, because success rarely comes to those who work for it. But it always comes to those who inherit it.

success affirmations

→ If I really believe I can succeed, then I am probably running a fever or still in the fourth grade.

→ Failure usually means I'm doing everything wrong.

→ Only three things can make me successful: luck, a big salary, or an inheritance.

→ If I'm doing my best and still not winning, then I'm only good enough to be where I am right now.

→ Dreams usually end the same way—the moment I wake up.

→ I can have anything I want in this life if I'm willing to lie, cheat, or do things that might be considered wrong.

→ If I could live my life over, I'm pretty sure I'd choose to be a lot more successful next time.

reality check

Take a good look at all the things
that helped to get you where you are today,
and then stop doing them.

chapter five

attitude

How come nobody wants to argue with me?
Is it because I am always so right?
—JIM BOUTON

When I was little, my mom thought I was smart as a whip. Even before I attended kindergarten and acquired the kind of knowledge and wisdom you'd expect from a public school education, she was asking me things I didn't know how to answer. She'd ask, "How many times have I told you not to do that?" I would respond with something like, "I don't know, you know how bad I am with math." She would just smile and spank me as if it were my birthday, even though it wasn't. She was kind of forgetful like that.

But the question she invariably asked over and over was, "Hey, where's that attitude coming from?" Afraid of guessing wrong, I would innocently ask, "I don't know, why don't you tell me where you think it's coming from?" I obviously needed help.

As I got older, she eventually grew weary of asking me these questions again and again—except the one about my attitude. As a matter of fact, I have friends to this day who still ask me about it. So I got on the Internet to see if I could find some answers.

Attitudes first appeared around 5000 BC in a small and fiercely defiant clan known as *Humanus toddlerus*. Anthropologists believe the *Humanus toddlerus* developed an attitude for one important reason. It broke down the *Humanus adultus* until the tantrum-throwing *Humanus toddlerus* was given a cheap plastic toy. Impressed with these results was a marauding and ruthless tribe known as *Humanus teenagerus*. Already surviving on a diet of apathy and indifference, the *Humanus teenagerus* eventually rose to power and developed a considerable attitude while working in fast-food restaurants and multiplex cinemas.

Attitude eventually splintered into two opposing forces. One was good; the other was not so good. It's unclear why the division was necessary when fundamentally their philosophies were very similar. A good attitude is about looking at life and saying, "Man, it doesn't get any better than this." A bad attitude is about looking at life and saying, "Man, it doesn't get any better than this."

But that's where the similarities end.

Good attitudes are a lot like taking laxatives. Too little does you no good at all. Too much, and you may be worse off than if you had just left well enough alone. Needless to say, losers neither endorse nor endure good attitudes—and for good reason. It's a little phony walking around with a good attitude while you're being used, stepped on, and treated like a redheaded pack mule. A good attitude may get you out of bed in the morning, but if rush hour hasn't crushed your spirit, clearly your alarm clock hasn't really gone off yet.

no, you can't

Actually, there's only one job on earth that requires a good attitude. It's called volunteering. If you want to help out and work and not be paid for it, knock yourself out. It's gonna take a good attitude to forget about how much you're working and how little you're being paid to do it. In fact, you better hope your good attitude will keep you from getting really mad when you realize that all of your unpaid time could have been spent doing something you actually enjoy doing.

One more thing—it's true that having a good attitude will probably not get you fired, but it doesn't make you Miss Spokesperson for the rest of us either.

Is there anything worse than having a good attitude? Yeah, there is. It's having a bad attitude. All a bad attitude will get you is the blame for things you never did. It's a magnet for it. And believe it or not, a bad attitude can—and will—get you fired. Just like stealing. It's that serious. Even those of us who lose all the time don't want to be associated with a bad attitude.

So, what do you do? You can't walk around pretending you enjoy being treated like a VCR at a garage sale. And you certainly don't want to be blamed for doing stupid, brainless, immature, or illegal things because somebody double-dog-dared you.

Remember the heartwarming story of my mom asking

where I got my attitude? Not where did I get my *good* attitude, or where did I get my *bad* attitude. Just—my attitude. I guess Mom had it figured out the whole time.

Children cannot choose to have good or bad attitudes. That's partly what makes them so spankable and gets them dropped off at Grandma's for the afternoon. We don't normally treat children like redheaded pack mules, and they're too immature to rely on their minds to stay calm when provoked. So they react impulsively with an "attitude." And since little kids are constantly testing boundaries with acts of defiance, we excuse their behavior and tolerate them having an attitude. Why? Because, they're four and they're cute.

So what is just having an "attitude"? An "attitude" is a manner of acting, feeling, or thinking that shows one's disposition to be defiant, disobedient, and combative. Boy, that sounds familiar, doesn't it? You bet it does. It's what we used to call having a bad attitude.

But wait, having a bad attitude is a bad thing—right? We can get fired for having a bad attitude. We go to therapy to try and conquer a bad attitude, don't we? That's right, we do. Believe me, in today's world, you don't want to be known for having a bad attitude. But having an "attitude" is perfectly acceptable.

So, what's the difference between having a "bad attitude" and having an "attitude"?

The difference is having a damn good reason. If you have a damn good reason to have a bad attitude, you no longer have a bad attitude. Now you have a justifiable, excusable, God-given right to behave in the manner you deem necessary when rules or results are not to your liking. Pretty incredible, huh? You are now a victim who has no other choice but to try to change things with defiant behavior—just like when you were four.

And when you have an attitude, you're no longer at fault when you're the one who started something, just like when you were four. In other words, when you perform or behave in a childlike manner to everyone around you, it's not only their fault, it's also about to be their problem.

An attitude is perfect in sports. Try having one *after* you do any of the following.

- **Make a foul**
- **Make a point**
- **Make bail**

Having an attitude is about demanding respect. Some people require a few other more trivial qualities be shown before respect is given—such as modesty or humility. These people are called dumb people, and dumb people also experience limitations of hearing and sight. When you find yourself in the presence of dumb people, remember to speak in a loud volume right in their face so that they are able to see *and* hear you.

Is there a better combination than making a lot of money and having an attitude to go with it? No, there is not. Everyone will know immediately that you are somebody who has a lot of money and wants everyone to know it. That's when you'll get all the respect you deserve.

What about the rest of us who don't make a lot of money? Can having an attitude be helpful or beneficial? You better believe it. In fact, the closer you are to minimum wage, the more helpful having an attitude can be. Let's find out how.

Have you eaten at a fast-food restaurant lately? Sure, the food is delicious, but believe me, you'll come back for the service. If the formula for success really is 90 percent attitude and 10 percent aptitude, then fast-food restaurants are currently staffed with a bunch of future Bill Gateses. Apparently, the only effective means of protecting oneself from irreparable harm from working a minimum-wage job is having an attitude about it. Does working fast food make you a loser? No. Does displaying the bare minimum of effort and courtesy to match the wage make you a loser? I'd say you're in the ballpark, yes.

The problem is that losers tend to be patronized and

exploited more than anybody else. So when employers are under the delusion they can hire you to work for twelve dollars an hour and expect a fifteen-dollar-an-hour amount of effort, it's your duty to turn in a six-dollar-an-hour amount of care and concern. It maintains the balance. An attitude is the great equalizer when expectations border on the bare minimum.

It's one reason why companies don't refer to their employees anymore as a "workforce." Nowadays, employees are part of a "team." That's because people on a team don't work together—they play together. You never hear the phrase "team worker," but you will hear "team player." Clever, huh? Listen, anytime you hear your employer mention anything about wanting you to play on a winning team, it means you're getting ready to be played all right—for a sucker.

An attitude lets customers know that you are being paid just to be there, not to appear as though you're thankful you have a job, and certainly not to display a cheery, helpful tone. Chances are you'd rather not even be there, right? The fact that you showed up to work at all should be respected and appreciated, but it rarely is. Sometimes the customers even act like they'd like to be appreciated—like they're doing you a favor by eating there. The only way to nip that attitude in the bud is to get your attitude out there first. Remember, the best defense is always offense.

An attitude also lets your employer know that you're there to be paid in exchange for doing what you absolutely have to do. Take it from me, you don't make any more on a minimum-wage gig when you multitask. If you're assigned to take food orders, there's no Christmas bonus for doing anything more than taking food orders. When you cover or fill in for another employee who is sick or late, you've opened up a can of worms. An employer will look to you as the go-to guy next time the staff is shorthanded.

Remind your employer it's not your name outside on the marquee. That should minimize any future requests regarding extra shifts.

Smart losers know the game. They see the angles. They see the big picture more than most. The longer you're a loser, the easier it is to recognize the flaws in the system. Losers know the odds are stacked against them. Just look at the number of minimum-wage employees versus the number of overpaid managers in any given company. Not a lot of room at the top, is there? It's the many versus the few. Always has been, always will be. Losers know that no matter how helpful they are, no matter how cheery they are, no matter how much they hustle, tomorrow is another day at the bottom of the food chain.

Beware of the following "team building" lies employers use to manipulate suckers:

- **Your job is entry level.**
- **Your minimum-wage job is a stepping-stone.**
- **This job is a great character builder.**
- **Work is its own reward.**

Please.

Or how about this phrase: "If you don't like your altitude, try changing your attitude." The implication, of course, is that your attitude is preventing you from reaching great heights. Oh really? See if this phrase doesn't make more sense: "My attitude is the result of not being able to reach great heights for reasons too difficult to overcome or change."

And if you're still banking on a good attitude to get you through life, let me say this right now: a good attitude plus eight bucks and change may get you a cup of coffee at Starbucks, but it won't buy you a promotion or a raise. Those are given to the employees who are. . .

A. Always willing
B. Always prepared
C. To kiss hindquarters

Your only real chance for high-altitude advancement is maintaining a handful of excuses that make you the victim and make everyone else appear arrogant, oppressive, stubborn, dense, or vengeful. When raises and promotions pass you by, try marching into your boss's office and explaining that the reason you haven't hit any of your sales targets is because India and China never signed on to NAFTA and are playing by their own rules. If that raises an eyebrow, then explain that your lack of focus lately is from a painful urinary infection that you've been too embarrassed to seek help for because of your secret "dual citizenship" down there.

A loser knows that the truth will, indeed, set you free. So always be ready with good excuses. Any excuse is legitimate, as long as it sounds better than the truth.

Also, feel free to switch excuses when the first one wears a little thin. Remember, if changing your attitude doesn't work, try changing excuses. When you can do that, you don't have to worry if your attitude is really making a difference and getting you noticed.

It is.

attitude affirmations

→ A good attitude may not get me fired, but it doesn't make me little Miss Spokesperson for everyone else.

→ A good attitude is like taking a laxative. Too much, and I may be worse off than if I hadn't taken any at all.

→ My only real obstacle in life is a bad attitude. And being mad about the things I don't have. And being angry about other people's success. Other than that, my only real obstacle in life is a bad attitude.

→ When changing my attitude doesn't work, I should try changing excuses.

→ Quitting has nothing to do with having a bad attitude. Quitting only means I'm ending my non-winning streak.

→ The only effective means of protecting myself from the irreparable harm of a minimum-wage job is having an attitude about it.

→ The only job on earth that requires me to have a good attitude is called volunteering.

chapter six

hope

Hope is delicate suffering.

—IMAMU AMIRI BARAKA

ope. I love the sound of that word. I have a niece named Hope. Her name is as beautiful as she is.

But not everyone has a pretty niece named Hope. They think hope is a way of summoning luck or divine intervention to bring them everything from winning lottery tickets to better health. They fill their hearts with hope and then, more often than not, wind up unhappy and disappointed. They even claim hope is what makes the world go round, which I think most scientists would argue against.

The hopeful say that if you have it, you have everything. They believe that hope can make all of your tomorrows better than your yesterdays. I agree with that. Your future can be better than your past, as long as you didn't hope for much yesterday.

If you're still one of these hopeful types, I probably sound a bit cynical. But nothing could be farther from the truth.

I do believe in hope. I believe hope is all you really have when you don't have enough money for an attorney. I believe hope is what you need when you genuinely lack talent or ability. I believe hope is a pretty face in the other car writing down your license number and desperately calling the Department of Transportation to find out who you are so she can date you. If that's not hope, I don't know what it is.

For most people, the problem with hope is that it leads to unrealistic expectations. Once you figure out that hope is a far cry from reality, you can trick yourself into believing your ex really would enjoy hearing from you at three in the morning when you're hammered. But don't worry—desperate phone calls in the middle of the night are not going to ruin your life. In fact, one or two of them might actually pay off.

No, the real problem with hope is that it leads to dream chasing. Dream chasing is a dangerous business. I'm not suggesting you give up your dreams; I'm only suggesting you give up on the idea of actually reaching them. You probably already believe all your dreams are somehow and in some way coming true—for someone else. That's why you're doing two things: obsessing over the things you don't have, and working a job you hoped you'd never have to do.

If you want to make your life twice as hard as it already is, start hoping for a dream that will, in all likelihood, never come true. If you're already doing that, my guess is you're walking around right now a pretty unhappy camper. Not unhappy in a manic-depressive kind of way—unhappy in an envious-of-others, dreading-the-holidays kind of way.

Even so, never forget that anything is possible—as long as you have hope.

Okay, I'm just kidding. That was a test. Do you see how vulnerable you are? Do you see how ready you are to be disappointed? When you even hear or see the word *hope,* your body releases chemicals that manipulate your brain into believing any kind of mumbo-jumbo that will supposedly make you happier or richer or healthier or whatever. That's why you'll sit and watch infomercials at 2 a.m. and believe that a few spare hours a month could turn you into a wealthy land baron. Watch those ads enough and you'll eventually order the tapes. It's not your fault. That's just hope messing with your mind.

Hope is like a crutch. Once you start relying on it, you'll be too afraid to make a move without it. Crutches are only good for two things: getting awesome parking at the mall and sympathy dates with hot chicks. Otherwise, they'll just slow you down.

But I'll tell you what you can hope to have when you're completely hopeless: *nothing.* Nothing, that is, if you call living a life without failures, faults, or defeats "nothing."

Hope is really nothing more than a dangerous bunch of expectations in disguise holding kitchen knives to your throat and demanding you either give them what they want or you'll end up a miserable failure. Hope is what tricks you into leaving your front door unlocked at night because you want to believe the world is a safe place. But by morning, you'll wake up and find all the cash in your purse has been replaced with a bunch of losing lottery tickets. Thanks, hope.

The fact is, there is a wall standing between you and eternal happiness, and that wall is called hope. Hope makes you believe you still have a chance when you really don't, and pretending you still have a chance is what makes you vulnerable, insecure, and uncertain. Well, you'll never be happy dealing with that much anxiety, so you've got to tear down that wall of hope. And I'm going to help you do it.

Let's say you're shooting hoops down at the Y and Michael Jordan invites you to play a little one-on-one. Just you and Michael playing basketball together. Would you do it? Of course you would. Would you expect to win? Nuh-uh. Any chance of scoring any points at all? Nope. Are you the least bit scared about it? Not at all.

Hmmm, not scared, no chance of scoring, no expectations of winning, and yet, having the time of your life. How can this be? You're having fun for one reason only: you have no hope of winning. None. You're having the best time because you know the situation is hopeless. Winning or losing does not matter to you, so you're having a blast while you're getting trounced, humiliated, embarrassed, and defeated.

Now, imagine your next sale, your next interview, or your next blind date without having any hope of getting the deal, getting the job, or getting to first base. This time, however, you're not disappointed about it. Not because you failed, but because you knew you didn't stand a chance. And without hope, you *don't* stand a chance.

I want you to do something. Starting tomorrow, try to imagine Michael Jordan is everywhere waiting to play a little one-on-one with you. Every opportunity, every problem, everyone at work, and every customer you meet—they're all Michael Jordan. You're going one-on-one and you don't stand a chance.

The funny thing is, Michael Jordan is not really expecting much out of you either. Why? Because he isn't wasting time and effort hoping he's going to win. More importantly, he's not wasting time hoping you're not good enough to win. Michael Jordan doesn't hope for results; he knows better. Michael Jordan knows sitting around and hoping for things will never make them come true.

Suddenly, the idea of giving up all hope doesn't seem so scary, does it? Hope is what heightens your expectations, leading to the attempts that cause your failures. If you don't have any expectations for yourself, and the world has no expectations for you, then you can never be at fault, never be blamed, and never be looked upon as a failure. Kill off hope and your life will never be the same—I promise. Remember, you can't be a failure when you have no hope of winning.

hope affirmations

→ Hope is all I have when I don't have enough money for an attorney.

→ Hope is what bypasses reality and leads me to believe things are not as they really are.

→ When I lose hope, I give up ever facing another disappointing loss.

→ I prove every day that high hopes lead to unhappy endings, because every day I go to a job I had high hopes I would never have to do.

→ If I really want to make my life twice as hard as it already is, I should start hoping for a dream that will, most likely, never come true.

→ Hope is nothing more than dangerous expectations in disguise.

→ I can't be a failure when I have no hope of winning.

reality check

Whoever said nothing is easy
has never tried quitting.

chapter seven

money

I don't want money. It is only people who
pay their bills who want that
and I never pay mine.
—OSCAR WILDE

oney. They say the love of it is the root of all evil. Maybe, but to suggest money can't buy happiness has never been asserted by anyone whose last name rhymes with Rockefeller, Carnegie, Gates, or Zuckerberg. If money can't buy happiness, then why in the heck is everyone peeing on themselves while jumping up and down and screaming for joy when they win money on TV game shows? Trust me, if you're penniless and jumping up and down in a wet diaper— and you're happy—you're either two years old, or you just yelled "Bingo!" in the nursing home.

The honest truth about money is this: somewhere lurking in your DNA is a chromosome that determines three things: how you will make money, how much of it you will make, and what you'll do with it after you make it. It's genetics alone that ultimately separates people who have a lot of money from the rest of us.

I don't want to waste a lot of time covering all the ways there are to make money. Besides, if you're relying on me at all for career guidance, you're in bigger trouble than you know. I will say that whatever it is you do for a living, you probably had a pretty good idea going in what it paid. If you're frustrated about it now because you sort of conveniently forgot, you should run it by an attorney to see if you have a case.

Don't get me wrong, I'm all for free enterprise. But does it seem a tad unfair that something as simple as choosing a career makes such a difference in income? A friend from high school chose to be a cardiologist and I chose not to be one. Okay, so he deserves to make twenty times more in a year than I do as a part-time musician? Why is there such an income disparity between similar-sounding jobs such as train engineer and electrical engineer? And why does a first-year lawyer at a firm make a heck of a lot more than a twelve-year receptionist at a veterinarian clinic?

It's not that some of us are unable to pursue normal careers or maintain what banks like to call "real jobs." It's just that the unusual or alternative professions seem to attract a personality more suited for flexible hours and inconsistent pay. Take all the musicians, actors, and writers in the world, throw in a few thousand homespun entrepreneurs, and you've got all the waiters and bartenders $2.15 an hour can buy.

Since there's not a car salesman alive who would ask himself this question, I will: Are there right ways and wrong ways to make a living? While tomorrow's history books sort all that out, keep in mind that—at least where making money is concerned—there is a big gray area between what's illegal and what's ingenious.

I will go on record now and say this for anyone who thinks it's okay to make a living engaging in the world's oldest profession: if you can sleep at night after making a living meeting with complete strangers and selling them condominium timeshares, that's your choice. But if laws can be passed to allow people to do that, then why can't we legally change the name of our country to the United States of Las Vegas so we can all enjoy a steak-and-egg breakfast for $1.99?

And to anyone who is hoping to strike it rich gambling, I have two important things to say. First, if you've ever used an ATM in a casino to withdraw cash because you knew the table that just took all of your money was fixin' to get hot, then there's nothing in this book you don't already know. Second, make sure you always keep the deeds and titles to your house and cars on you, or you'll be kicking yourself the next time you're in the middle of an unbelievable losing streak and need to bet big to win big.

Speaking of sound fiscal advice, did you know that owning your own home can mean not having to work for months—or even years? They're called "second mortgages" but honestly, they should be called "not-going-to-work-for-a-whileages." And yes, borrowing against the value of your home is tax deductible. The only deduction you can make from bringing home a regular paycheck is that you ain't bringing home very much.

So where does this leave you financially? Probably trying to figure out how to make more money at your current job that you no longer enjoy doing, while you're wishing you made more money doing something else you're not qualified to do. It's what scientists call the Big Dang Theory, and it's how your universe began its downward spiral.

The real focus of this chapter is on how you can live as if you were making the kind of money you think you oughta be making. After all, there are only three things you can do with money: save it, invest it, or spend it. Is doing more of one better than doing less of another? You better believe it.

Saving money sounds like a good idea, doesn't it? Actually, it isn't. First, you can never save enough—*ever*. Whatever you think will be enough, won't be. And it's a bad omen. It's like Murphy's Law in reverse. Whatever you save will be matched by a serious problem costing at or more than the relative value. In other words, save it and you're just begging to blow out a knee or an engine—it'll happen. Only this time, you brought it all on yourself. Besides, if you can't take it with you, then what are you holding onto it for? Emergencies? No, that's what credit cards are for. Health care? No, that's what Medicare is for. Retirement? Listen, do you know what you do when you retire? You sit around waiting to die. Boring.

But don't worry, you won't be sitting around long according to statistics. You'll be doing yourself the biggest favor by removing that flimsy savings net from under your golden years. And later, when all your retired friends are sitting around dying, you'll be enjoying a nice meal at McDonald's—on your shift break.

What about investing? Well, if you're not one for playing the lottery or betting on the ponies, you're not gonna like investing much either. There are simply no guarantees in life—none. If you invest your money, you could lose it all. The market calls it an "adjustment." Auditors for Enron called it "embezzling." You will call it "poverty." And all you're gonna wish is that you had spent it on something frivolous so you had something to show for it.

Can you invest and make money? Sure, it's possible, but it's a long shot. It's like sending money to a TV preacher hoping it's enough to lower your cholesterol. And think about this: whatever you save or whatever you make investing will ultimately be ripped apart and shredded by vultures and hyenas, which are Australian words for *taxes* and *kids*.

That leaves us with the only thing you should be doing with your money, and that's spending it as fast as you can make it.

Again, we come back to this silly notion of money not

being able to buy happiness. Well, only someone with money who didn't want you to rob them of it would say such a thing. Of course money buys you happiness. You've seen with your own eyes how happy people are who have it. Good grief, that's why they *are* happy and the quicker you acknowledge and accept that, the easier it becomes to use whatever means are necessary to make money.

Tell me what would make you happier—being on the phone with a creditor or being on the phone making reservations for an Alaskan cruise? Would you rather be sharing a cold Bud with your neighbor in his garage or sharing a cold Bud with your neighbor's wife ringside in Las Vegas? Besides, where's the harm in having a few nice things that impress the kind of people who would never be friends with you otherwise?

Do you know what the world's most condescending phrase is? I'll give you a hint: it starts with the word *delayed* and ends with the word *gratification*. If I had to wait until I could afford everything I wanted, I'd be living no better than a public school teacher. Who wants to live like that? Most teachers have to stay after school and aren't paid for the extra time they're having to sit there. Isn't that how we punish the bad students?

And next time some Rockefeller-type utters some lame-brain advice about making out a budget and sticking to it, tell him you don't make enough to live on a budget.

There are a couple of expressions I do like. How about "Life is short" or "You can't take it with you"? I have another—it's called "approved credit." The fact is, most of us are always gonna owe somebody something anyway, whether it's Uncle Sam, the bank, or a bookie. Just knowing about things like your own mortality and how happy you are owning things other people don't have is all the more reason to take full advantage of having approved credit.

Sadly, what you do for a living will determine how much money you make. But thank goodness what you make doesn't necessarily determine how much you are able to spend. The thing you do need to be cautious about is not pushing your credit cards over their limits—simultaneously. You don't want to paint yourself into a corner with five or ten maxed-out cards. *Then* what would you be able to afford? And you never want to pay more than 18 to 21 percent in interest. If you are, stop charging for every little thing you want and only charge for the things you need.

Here's a good rule of thumb: "needs" are things you have to have like groceries, gasoline, HD TV's, and Starbucks. "Wants" are things you put off buying until you really need them. The thing about money is that you're always gonna want more than you have. *Always.* Well, if the money is never going to be enough anyway, why worry? That's the whole point of having credit.

One last thing about money and good advice: early to bed and early to rise may make you healthy and wise, but it will not make you wealthy. Again, that requires a really good salary—or an inheritance.

Losers are actually very anxious and devoted to making money faster than anyone. I can tell you from years of experience investing in get-rich-quick schemes that have yet to pay off, that there is still no faster, easier way to make money. So if you are ever approached about an opportunity that suggests you will make a lot of money in a hurry, you'd be a fool to put one dollar in on an obvious scam when putting in every dollar you own could make you so much more money.

Be a loser with your cash and you'll never again have to worry about investments or savings or having enough to retire on. Playing fast and loose with your money promises one thing no long-term savings plan can offer you: guaranteed results.

money affirmations

→ When I try to save money, I'm only inviting an unexpected catastrophe that will wipe me out of every dime I've saved.

→ There is no harm in buying shiny things on credit that make others envious of me.

→ Going to bed early and getting up early will not make me wealthy. Being paid a really good salary will make me wealthy.

→ I'm going to find people who inspire me and ask them if they would mind giving me money instead.

→ Making good money always overrides doing the right thing.

→ Folks with cash get great deals. Folks without cash get approved credit.

→ Second mortgages and casino gambling are great sources of income.

→ Money used for saving and investing is money I'll never see again. That money gets split between my taxes and my kids.

chapter eight

cheating

Everybody has a little Watergate in him.

—BILLY GRAHAM

heating. Where there's a will, there's always a way. Somebody wrote a book years ago—some nonsense about never needing to know more than what you learned in kindergarten. Well, if that were really true, I guess you could take one of your finger paintings down to the bank and use it to secure a car loan. Trust me, the real world requires you have a little more than a kindergarten education, unless you're a hand model.

I think I'll call my next book *All You Need to Know You Can Learn in High School.* That's the real age of discovery. One of the first things I learned to do in high school was procrastinate. Why not put off until tomorrow what never would've gotten done today anyway? Only fools rush in where losers have already tread.

Punctuality is something else I learned about in high school. I learned that when you always show up on time, it's not appreciated—it's expected. Being fashionably late accomplishes two things: one, it challenges authority as to whether 9 a.m. sharp was intended for your time zone; two, it sends a message that you have bigger fish to fry. Being late to class or for work all the time is like saying, "I'm so ready not to be here anymore. Who's with me?" I think you'll be amazed how many others will be joining you.

But more vital than qualities such as patience and punctuality, the single most important skill I learned in high school was cheating. What I didn't know was how valuable that knowledge would come in handy in the real world.

But wait—cheating is something bad people do, isn't it? When you cheat you're only cheating yourself, aren't you? Hmm, sounds like somebody dropped out of school right after kindergarten.

The sad truth is, a lot of things our mothers and kindergarten teachers told us weren't true at all. Did your eyes stay crossed because you kept crossing them? Did you ever go blind looking at naked pictures? Did world famine end because you ate all your vegetables? The people who told you those things, though well intended, are the same people who taught you that cheating is bad and being patient and punctual are good.

So has being patient ever made you miss out on a really good bargain or a great opportunity? Probably. Did everlasting love ever slip through your fingers because you were being patient like a good little kindergartner? Sure it has.

What about all the good things you get for always trying to be on time? Have you ever gotten a speeding ticket? Have you ever had to wait forty-five minutes or more because you arrived as scheduled for a doctor's appointment?

Well, if patience and punctuality are sometimes not a good thing, why isn't cheating sometimes not a bad thing? In other words, how can cheating be wrong when so many people are doing it?

If you're like most folks, accepting the concept that cheating is a good thing will be an uphill battle. Because of some influential people in your life when you were young, you believe cheating is unethical, immoral, and wrong. Are there times when cheating is not only to your advantage— it's also the right thing to do? I think you already know the answer to that.

Think of cheating as a secret battle plan for taking down the enemy. And the secret to defeating the enemy and getting ahead is meeting your enemy halfway on a battlefield known as "A Really Gray Area." Now, don't confuse A Really Gray Area here with the "Gray Area" we discussed in the chapter on ethics. The differences are usually things only longtime losers can grasp or understand.

If you recall, the Gray Area is an invisible place where decisions and choices need to be justified. But A Really Gray Area is where the real battles in your life take place. The rules of engagement are less confusing in A Really Gray Area. It's a place where choices are never wrong and consequences are never judged. A narrow-minded, black-and-white view of the world is never allowed or tolerated in A Really Gray Area. In other words, a life dedicated to living in A Really Gray Area can turn a simplistic, kindergarten education into a high school chemistry class passed with flying colors.

Did you know that preparing for a test and being prepared for a test are two different things? Funnier still, our public schools offer classes that actually teach kids how to cheat. I know—I took one. Of course, they didn't call it "cheating," they called it "chemistry." But by the time the course was over, I knew everything there was to know about cheating.

And parents are the biggest supporters of cheating. How many parents ever see an A on a report card and ask their child if they cheated to get it? None. Kids take that as a wink and a nod that it's okay to cheat as long as they're smart enough to not get caught doing it. Some people might argue that it is wrong to graduate from school by any means necessary. Those people are called philosophy majors. And the only way you're gonna make money with a degree in philosophy is by pulling jury duty or giving blood a couple of times a week.

The rightness or wrongness of cheating is this: as long as you know in your heart that you wouldn't have had to cheat if you'd had more time to practice or prepare, then you're not really cheating. Why should you have to count your third golf stroke coming out of the woods when you know you wouldn't have been there in the first place if you'd had more time to practice? In other words, cheating allows you to do some incredible things with surprisingly little effort.

The only real negative to cheating is in getting caught. Believe me, if you're not smart enough to get away with it, you deserve to be caught. The shame alone will be your punishment. Okay, not really, but being caught will either make you a better cheater or at least qualify you to date a Kardashian.

If you do become proficient at it, I mean, if you take to cheating like a wealthy parent paying to inflate an SAT score for their academically challenged kid, you'll notice immediate improvements in everything from golf scores to tax refunds to "Hellooooo, Stanford." There are few things in life better for giving you an instant sense of accomplishment than cheating. And cheating can be such fun. Did you ever sneak into a drive-in movie via the trunk? (Note: if you're under the age of thirty or a philosophy major, skip down to the next paragraph.) Wasn't it thrilling to see if you could cheat and get away with it? Figuratively speaking, you can still have that sneaking-into-the-drive-in excitement when time is not on your side and you need to beef up your résumé for a job you're woefully underqualified to do.

As I mentioned earlier, I want to touch on the benefits of cheating in relation to justice. Cheating is one of the few times two wrongs can make a right. Let's say you receive income under the table (Wrong #1) that never gets reported (Wrong #2) and is, therefore, never taxed. Is that cheating, or is it justifiable and exactly what the IRS deserves for auditing you last year? The answer should be obvious.

So when you're ready to live where things aren't so difficult to do, where shortcuts and detours get you easily across the great dilemmas and around the unfair advantages others always seem to have, just pack up your troubles and head to a little town called Losersville. You can't miss it. Just cut though Cheaters Pass and don't stop until you find yourself in A Really Gray Area.

cheating affirmations

→ Cheating allows me to level an uneven playing field.

→ Cheating, when used in the pursuit of justice, is not only appropriate, it's ethical.

→ I wouldn't dare cheat if I didn't think I was smart enough to get away with it.

→ The upshot of cheating is immediate, noticeable results.

→ Whoever said, "When you cheat, you're only cheating yourself" never brought home all A's and received a black T-top Camaro from two very appreciative parents.

→ Cheating is like a garden that grows best in a shady place called A Really Gray Area.

→ I'm not proud of cheating my way through high school algebra to get an A, but the dean of admissions where I sent my transcript sure was impressed.

reality check

If you want nice things like a house, a luxury
car, and lots of money, you should work
really hard to find out if collecting your
inheritance early is even legal.

chapter nine

anger

I am free of all prejudice.
I hate everyone equally.

—W. C. FIELDS

uestion: When life keeps dumping on you, or when you have it a lot harder than the other guy, what choice do you have other than to be angry about it?

Answer: no @*%! choice whatsoever!

Anger is like cholesterol. One type is bad, the other type is good. Too much of the bad can kill you. Too much of the good will, uh—well, don't worry, you probably don't have too much of the good.

The human body is basically a sack of fluid and bones assimilating information. You convert that information into thoughts, and from those thoughts you experience emotions. Your emotions are merely reactions, called feelings, born of thoughts or physical sensations. You're not made, nor equipped, to acquire and store anything but information—and maybe some viruses and a few extra holiday pounds.

Pretty simple, right? If you think about that puppy you loved as a kid that mysteriously disappeared about the time that dog-hating tramp of a stepmom your dad married moved in, you feel sadness and anger. Think about an old flame who cheated on you and ran off with your best friend, and you just feel anger.

But you can't store those emotions, so you have to keep thinking about how nice it would be to get even with that two-faced, overweight, cheating liar. It's the same reason you still feel sadness and anger when you wonder if that puppy ever found another home where an evil tramp of a stepmom didn't mind his shedding and barking so much.

That's anger, all right. It's an emotion resulting from a thought. But if you try to store that anger, it will kill you. It will. You should never force your body to do something it was not made to do—like singing karaoke in front of your in-laws. It's just a bad idea.

So what do you do with your anger? You know how much you hate doing certain things and how much you dislike certain people. There's no avoiding how annoyed you get when you're inconvenienced, interrupted, cut off in rush hour, or made to wait. You've got good reasons to be angry; you just don't need to let it eat you up inside. Let the cigarettes and sugary snacks do that.

If you're one of the millions who have been misled by well-meaning parents and a few misguided psychologists, allow me to light a candle and lead you back to your dark side. Anger is nothing to be afraid of; it is only an emotion. Like joy—only just the opposite. When you feel anger, I guarantee you one of three things is happening: you are around somebody very stupid, you are driving behind somebody really slow, or you're playing golf. My guess would be that when you're in one of those situations, you're trying really hard not to show your anger. And managing your anger? Pfft, ridiculous. That's what shrinks want you to do. They call it "anger management." Could any two words be more contrary than *anger management?* Those two words go together like *cheap divorce, enjoyable flight,* or *supportive mother-in-law.* We need anger management about as much as we need joy management.

Anger is probably one of the more confusing emotions, but it doesn't have to be. I'm gonna help you not only to revel in it, but also to enjoy expressing it so often you'll wonder why you ever wasted time trying to suppress it—or worse, manage it.

First of all, having anger is not what makes you a loser. But, how you release your anger—ahhh, there's the rub.

Secondly, there are only two forms of anger: "Chihuahua anger" and "Cujo anger."

Chihuahua anger is as cute as it sounds. It barks, it bites, and it'll show its teeth, and it's so doggone lovable that nobody's really afraid of it. But it is released. It's Mom getting mad when you're up past your bedtime. It's you demanding to see a manager when a product or service is inferior. It's you whispering to Mr. LoudVoice talking on his cell that everyone in the theater would actually prefer the movie audio over hearing anything else about his day. Chihuahua anger is healthy, justified, necessary, protective, and appropriate. And for many people, it's enough.

But for the rest of us, it's not enough to let out a little steam gently when it's justified and appropriate. We don't walk around with a slightly irritated little Chihuahua inside of us. We live with a rabid, unstable Saint Bernard on our front porch—and a stranger just pulled up. We have Cujo anger, and that's what this chapter is really all about. There is simply nothing better than calling on Cujo to remedy life's little annoying situations.

How easy is it to release Cujo from his chain? As easy as one, two, *sic 'em.* Say you're at a grocery store and you're being held up in the checkout line by a little old lady digging in her purse for some pennies or pictures of her grandkids or whatever. First, try to speed things up by clearing your throat several times. If she can't hear you, which for her age wouldn't be a stretch, you might have to include some heavy sighs. If she still refuses to acknowledge you, then be a gentleman and offer to pay by tossing a nickel on the counter and asking her if that's what she's looking for. If she continues digging in her purse, let her know—in a volume you're pretty sure she can hear this time—that you would like to get home sometime today. That should speed things up a bit.

Thanks to Cujo, you've let the world know, or at least half the people in the store know, that your time is more valuable than anyone else's. Waiting in slow lines and fuming is a recipe for a heart attack or a stroke. Trying to manage or contain Cujo is useless. Remember, you don't feel anger when you're alone and just minding your own business. Unless, of course, you're playing golf.

The trick is to vent your frustrations when somebody is being insensitive and inconsiderate to your needs. Releasing Cujo on a moment's notice not only provides more opportunities to belittle slow or stupid people, but also offers you protection from clever people who think they can get away with doing something really stupid to you.

Of course, as with all things, moderation is the key. So the next time you yell or scream or get angry with people, remember to apologize immediately to avoid any resentment on their part. Then, if they do or say anything stupid again, they shouldn't be insulted because they know how easily upset you can get. Allowing Cujo out of his cage is always justified when you're pretty sure someone didn't listen or understand you the first time.

If you're just not the kind of person who is comfortable apologizing after you unleash a verbal assault, try this little trick: get all your anger out and then quickly say, "Oh, I'm just kiddin' ya." That way, if they say anything back to you, they'll look like a real jerk who can't take a joke. Meanwhile, everyone will be laughing at them and thinking that you are witty and fun to be around.

Now, just because you enjoy unhooking Cujo from his leash doesn't mean you're allowed to make threats. In today's PC world, always remember two things: cameras are everywhere, and no one will hesitate to turn you in for the reward.

Once you're comfortable allowing Cujo out whenever somebody pushes your buttons, you will start to notice a big difference in how people treat you. You'll be shown a level of respect you never thought possible. People will not only stare at you in amazement, they will also know they are standing before a mental giant and wouldn't dare cross verbal swords with the likes of you. Nobody likes to confront anger and they won't have the courage to challenge yours.

The underlying theme here is control—and that's what anger gives you. It's ironic that what society alleges is a lack of self-control, like anger, actually gives you a tremendous amount of control over others. That's why it's okay to call a complete stranger a moron. Or a numbskull. Or an idiot. Which brings me to my definition of Cujo anger. Cujo anger is justifiable verbal or physical self-defense against anyone who doesn't agree with you.

Demonstrating extreme, vicious, and hateful anger lets the other person know that your efforts and your results are not only superior to everyone else's, but they're also not likely to be improved, amended, or modified to suit anyone's liking but your own.

That is how you earn someone's respect.

Cujo anger is a lot like driving a big Hummer down a crowded street. Trust me, everyone will get out of your way. You just have to have the courage to hop in and smash down on the accelerator. If you try to hold it in, that's when you start doing the real damage to your body that pork chops and white gravy were meant to do.

Your Cujo anger cannot be managed. It cannot be redirected. It cannot be reassigned. It cannot be repressed.

It must be released or it will come out in other ways, making you say and do the most unforgivable and embarrassing things. You'll wake up the next day with that sick feeling in your gut wondering who that wild, spitting, hollering madman was last night singing karaoke in front of the in-laws.

anger affirmations

→ My anger is always justified when I'm around slow or stupid people, or when I'm playing golf.

→ Anger management is an oxymoron. I need it about as much as I need joy management.

→ When life keeps dumping on me, what choice do I have other than to be angry all the time?

→ If someone gets angry with me for cutting in line, I'll just explain to them that I get just as angry when I have to wait in line.

→ I can't profess to be a kind and loving mate one minute and the next become verbally abusive—unless they kind of had it coming.

→ A good example of carrying around anger is telling someone I hope I never see them again and then stalking them.

→ My anger is always justified if they didn't listen or understand me the first time.

→ It's okay to get really angry at anyone who disagrees with me.

chapter ten

forgiveness

It is a common delusion that you make things
better by talking about them.

—DAME ROSE MACAULAY

h, forgiveness. Humanity's eternal hope. It is the greatest gift we can give to each other and to ourselves. It is the common denominator.

Forgiveness cannot be corrupted. Its value and purpose is something we all understand. It is perhaps the one thing that winners and losers do exactly the same, right?

Almost.

Losers not only find clever ways to shirk responsibility, they quickly figure out how to turn courageous and honorable deeds into involuntary acts of impropriety. Even forgiveness cannot escape the unbelievable difference a loser's touch can make.

I've discovered over the years that forgiveness is like a foreign language for some people. They don't speak it and they don't understand it. And without fail, the ones who don't give it are the ones who don't get it. It's disheartening to know that something so universal, so loving, so beautiful as the word *forgiveness* can be so misused and so misunderstood.

And to forgive is so simple, so easy to do. Maybe the problem is that we've forgotten how to forgive. Or maybe it's that our pride sees forgiveness as a sign of weakness when, of course, nothing could be farther from the truth. Apart from handing over a fully furnished summer home on the coast of Maui, forgiveness is the most generous gift you can give somebody.

Take a moment and think about how easy it is to really forgive someone—or yourself. And seeking forgiveness can be just as easy—if you know how. Maybe a little refresher course would help, so let's start with the basics: How do you seek forgiveness from someone so they know you're being thoughtful and sincere?

Here's how: the next time you make a horrible mistake, rectify it immediately with an apology. If that doesn't work, see if a hundred bucks will cover it.

Now how hard was that? We all know talk is cheap. Verbal apologies are little more than a bunch of words strung together. But flashing a wad of cash lets the person you've hurt or insulted know that you're prepared to make things all better again. You've got something more powerful than an apology. You've got cash. You're gonna slip the offended a C-note— perhaps two C-notes depending on their level of anger. And then you're gonna wait for your hug or a thank-you or possibly even an apology when they realize they were probably being a little too sensitive to begin with. People prefer cash over apologies anyway. Why else would we need so many lawyers?

Now, don't get me wrong. If a simple apology will suffice, by all means, look them in the eye and start slobbering about how wrong you were or whatever. Throw in some tears if you think it'll help. But if you need that little extra sentimental something, then whip out your checkbook. You won't believe the heartfelt response you're about to get.

Some people might consider the one-hundred-dollar gesture to be rude and offensive. Some would even call it a bribe or a payoff. That's ridiculous. I mean, it's only a hundred bucks. And I assure you, a hundred bucks alone won't usually cut it. You'll still have to throw in a few "I'm sorry's" and a tearful "It won't happen again."

But what a hundred bucks can do is let them know that you are willing to put your money where your mouth is. And once they accept your apology or cash offer, they're letting you know they'll never breathe a word about this to anybody. In fact, it'll kind of be like the whole thing never happened, and isn't that what forgiveness is all about?

So cry with them, make excuses, promise you'll never do whatever, ever again. Just make sure you say it while you slip a folded one-hundred-dollar bill into their shirt pocket or purse. And whatever you do, make sure they see you do it so that you get full credit. It's the only way they can be sure that you're sincere and that you care.

forgiveness affirmations

→ When I make a horrible mistake, I should rectify it immediately with an apology. But if an apology alone is not accepted, I'm gonna see if a hundred bucks will smooth things over.

→ I will always make sure the people I'm forced to apologize to actually witness me slipping the hundred bucks into their shirt pocket or purse so they'll know I'm sincere.

→ Most people are usually oversensitive when their feelings get hurt, so I will never apologize unless I'm absolutely certain that I have to see the person again.

reality check

Next time a friend or loved one says they expected
more from you, tell them they should've thought
about that before they loaned you the money.

chapter eleven

work

They say hard work never hurt anybody,
but I figure why take the chance?

—RONALD REAGAN

read in the paper last week about a professional football player suspended for two games because he was caught with an illegal substance in his possession. His two-game salary loss: $308,000. That is not a typo. That is $154,000 a game, or $154,000 a week if it makes you feel any better. To be fair, those numbers are gross, football is a seasonal sport, and he is not the highest-paid player in the league.

In the context of this book, however, I would just like to clarify what I mean when I say the word *work*. I consider work to be anything you never did as a kid just for fun. Yes, I'm aware many of our adult postal carriers probably played post office as little boys and little girls. But I'll bet working for the post office as an adult isn't anything like playing post office when we were kids. Let's all pray I'm right about that.

The work I'm referring to in this chapter is the kind of work you either have to do, hate to do, or aren't being paid enough to do. If your work fits all three categories, this chapter is for you.

Thomas Edison once said, "Opportunity is missed by most people because it is dressed in overalls and looks like work." I don't know. I wouldn't say I've missed too many opportunities dressed like that. In fact, anything wearing overalls and looking like work is not something I'd say I miss very often at all.

And therein lies one of the great myths about losers—that losers shy away from opportunities. Losers *don't* shy away from opportunities. In fact, losers are always hard at work looking for the next great opportunity. Ask the people you work with who works the hardest, and losers are usually the first to raise their hands. Losers aren't afraid to admit they work twice as hard for half the pay. And they're pretty keen about noticing who's getting twice the pay for doing half the work. But do losers complain? Sure, but how else are we supposed to make a difference?

The trouble, I believe, is a simple misunderstanding about everyone's job description. First of all, you're either the boss or you're not. Most of us are not. So if you're the employee, your job is to make your boss's job easier. Your boss's job is to make more money doing his job than you make doing your job.

Survival at any job is a snap if you'll remember to do one thing: never speak until spoken to. If someone at work is nervous because they think they're about to be fired, just give them a reassuring pat on the back and tell them they're probably right. When your boss blames you for a mistake she made, thank her and tell her she deserves all the credit. Believe me, years from now you'll remember all the times your boss looked to you when things went wrong. You never really forget someone who treats you with that level of respect.

Of course, being an agreeable person at work does not mean you have to get along with everyone. Salaries and titles determine who gets a smiley "good morning" and who barely gets a nod. Even if you wake up and discover you're in a dead-end job and you've been doing little more than trading time for a skimpy paycheck, try not to let your bitterness and low self-esteem earmark you as deadweight, unproductive, and generally uncooperative. You don't want people to think that you're in management, do you?

Now, here's the good news. There is simply nothing else on earth that can make you look forward to working fifty to sixty hours a week other than your own troubled marriage. And if your spouse has been cheating on you, then trust me, you'll actually enjoy going to work every day. Wishing every morning you were anywhere other than having breakfast with that killjoy is the best medicine for making sure you're never too sick to make it into work each and every day.

So think about your job right now and the people you work with. Would you say you're on a team full of losers, or do you think you're hanging out with some real winners? If you're like most people, you'd probably say you're strapping on your helmet and playing mental rugby with a bunch of losers. The question is, are you the team captain?

And the work itself—is it boring and redundant? Does it feel like the outcome is exactly the same day after day, no matter how poorly you're playing the game? Well, guess what? Work is a rigged game; it has been from day one. Your path down the loser brick road is guided and controlled by two forces spawned from your extensive history of temp jobs, botched interviews, and unmarketable skills. I'm referring to *expectations* and *discouragement*.

Expectations are those cute little sparkly things in your eyes at the job interview. They're the butterflies you feel on your first day on the job. Look around tomorrow when you get to work. Do you laugh to yourself at the new employee who still seems hopelessly idealistic? Does it take you back to the time when you thought you were going to conquer the impossible and accomplish what had never been done before?

You know better now, though, don't you? You have *experience*, which is a fancy word for bitterness. You found out a long time ago there really isn't an *i* in team and blah blah whatever else. If there's one thing experience has taught you, it's never to pull away from the herd. You'll end up being hunted down and killed off by one of your own.

Discouragement is just the culmination of years of frustration, rejection, and defeat all bottled up into one dose of reality you chug from a shot glass that's always half empty. If you still aren't discouraged after months or years of getting nowhere on the job, seek out anyone who's more dedicated to losing than you. They'll explain why things don't change and why you'll never get ahead. And never seek the counsel of discouragement without bringing coffee and donuts. Caffeine and sugar will drag the truth out of anybody.

Discouragement is very easy to recognize. It's usually waiting for you in the employee break room. Discouragement smartens you up by pulling others in on projects so that when things go wrong you'll have someone else to blame. When you have enough experience being really discouraged, you'll be so clever at hiding it that no one will know if you're incompetent or just indifferent.

If you currently rank among the unemployed, then you not only know the meaning of the word *nap*, you also know the names of all the TV models on *The Price Is Right*. You also know that the only thing worse than having a job is looking for one. Going out to find work is like fetching your momma a switch so she can whip you with it. Having to search for something that always ends up hurting you is emotionally brutal, and all your whining and crying never seems to ease the pain. Thankfully, my momma couldn't stand the thought of me hating her, so she would always give me cookies after a whipping. That's how companies apologize when you get a job—except they use paychecks.

If you are having trouble getting a job and you're getting turned down a lot, it might not be your presentation at all. It could be your lack of preparation, your attitude, your lack of experience, or your inability to conceal your incompetence.

One final thought regarding hard work and hoarding pennies away for your so-called retirement. They say time flies when you're having fun, so if you work hard and save a pile of money to enjoy a work-free retirement, your sunset years will be over before you can say "Miami Beach." But if you skip the hard-work part and focus more on the having-fun part, then your skimpy nest egg will make your retirement years feel like they're never ending.

work affirmations

→ Those who can, do. Those who can't, teach. Those who can't do or teach become managers and take 20 percent from those who can.

→ My job is to make my boss's job easier. My boss's job is just the opposite of my job.

→ The best incentive to get up and go to work every day is an unhappy marriage.

→ If I do something nice for a customer without expecting a favor in return, then I must be a dog, a goldfish, or just someone not cut out for automobile sales.

→ Salaries and titles determine who I have to get along with at work and who I don't.

→ I should never attempt to do projects alone so I'll always have someone other than myself to blame.

chapter twelve

regret

Murder is always a mistake. One should never do
anything one cannot talk about after dinner.

—OSCAR WILDE

egret. A lot of fuss is made over that word. *Guilt* is another one. In fact, people waste more time and money dealing with guilt and regret than they do at Starbucks waiting for their super venti white mocha latte cha cha cha brûlée.

Why? You can't get rid of regret and guilt any more than you can get back the time and money you've spent on over-priced cups of beans, sugar, and water. That's the bad news. The good news is that deep regret and endless guilt are not only inevitable, they're tolerable—if you know how.

First, what doesn't work: therapy. Talking about problems all the time is like throwing fertilizer on weeds. It won't make any grass grow and it for sure won't kill the weeds, but it *will* kill a bunch of time and money.

Doing nothing also does not work. When someone claims they have few regrets in life, that's called *denial.* Denial works great in the short run but long term it's the wrong approach. Dealing with endless guilt and deep regret requires maturity, diligence, and not waiting for a pound of cure called therapy.

Real healing starts with only an ounce, or maybe just a half-ounce, of prevention.

To begin the healing process, try comparing the countless things you hate about yourself to harmless, everyday items. Regrets are like weeds. You may not have many, but if left untreated, they'll eventually choke out and kill everything in your yard, except for the trees.

Trees are like excuses. They're easy to lean against and provide plenty of shade for protection from the heat of the sun. The sun is like endless guilt. And on days when the sun (guilt) is extra hot, it helps to have trees (excuses) to lie under. It's no coincidence that you won't have as many weeds (regrets) when you have an abundance of trees (excuses). That's why we let trees (excuses) grow and don't cut them down unless we absolutely have to.

Like in-laws during the holidays, weeds (regrets) are impossible to get rid of and difficult to control. And if you don't have many trees (excuses), then odds are you're struggling with weeds (regrets) year after year. But you're in luck. There are two products proven to be highly effective against weeds (regrets). One is a liquid containing alcohol. The other is a chemical called drugs.

How effective are they? Well, many swear they'll never stop using them. And they work so fast that after only one or two applications you won't believe how good everything looks again. They may be applied separately or together, although one or the other is usually enough to do the trick. Combining the two can be extremely dangerous. But once you see the results, you'll wonder how you ever got along without them.

It bears repeating that the liquid containing the alcohol and the chemical called drugs will not eliminate weeds (regrets). Small doses, however, will make them less of a nuisance—at least temporarily. A consistent and daily application is necessary to combat recurring weeds (regrets). And because they're both concentrated, just a few ounces of each will go a long way. Long-term use is readily available and quite affordable.

As wonderful as all this sounds, the benefits of the liquid containing alcohol and the chemical called drugs are not widely endorsed. Many would have you believe that treatment should be left in the hands of a qualified professional. But who would you rather trust—trained professionals or millions of people who, just like you, are treating deeply rooted problems with quick and easy fixes?

Of course, nobody is immune to stupidity. Always use the liquid containing alcohol and the chemical called drugs carefully and in excessive moderation. And whatever you do, don't start applying one without first making sure you have suitable amounts of the other. You want to attack all of your weeds (regrets) in one application. If you run out before coverage is complete, you'll have wasted valuable time and money. And those are two things losers need no help in wasting.

I couldn't sleep tonight if I failed to mention a potentially serious problem regarding the care and handling of the liquid containing alcohol and the chemical called drugs. Never allow your friends to handle either one unless you are absolutely sure they are aware of the dangers. If they spill any on themselves on the drive home or run into a telephone pole, they might sue you—and they'll win, too. If clumsy coffee-spilling drivers, pop-star child molesters, and wife-killing professional athletes can win a jury over, then you don't stand a chance going up against a former friend who's mad at you for making them use bad judgment.

Weeds (regrets) are tough to treat. They are just some of the many things that never seem to change or go away or in any way improve your quality of life. They are simply tolerated and endured—like traffic jams and mothers-in-law. Thank goodness for shortcuts and no-contest divorces.

There is help out there. So don't be afraid to help yourself, as millions do every day. If you have deep regrets (weeds) and endless guilt (sunshine) and you're afraid death (relief) is still too far off, discover what distillers, chemists, and stressed-out soccer moms already know—that peace of mind is just a half-ounce to an ounce of prevention away.

regret affirmations

→ I can't get rid of regret and guilt any more than I can get back the money I've spent on pay-per-view wrestling.

→ Giving a therapist a hundred bucks to keep me from worrying about guilt works about as well as giving a policeman a hundred bucks to keep me from getting a speeding ticket.

→ When I say I don't have many regrets, that's not called a clear conscience. That's called denial.

→ Regret and guilt can never be managed. With regular doses of a liquid containing alcohol and a chemical called drugs, however, they can be tolerated.

→ Peace of mind is usually just a half-ounce to an ounce of prevention away.

reality check

You should never worry about
someone else's opinion of you, unless they
happen to be right.

chapter thirteen

criticism

Since we have to speak well of the dead,
let's knock them while they're alive.

—JOHN SLOAN

riticism. You're either dishing it out or you're having to take it. Losers are capable of doing a good bit of both, but what is it about criticism that separates winners from losers?

The answer is that winners tend to be more critical of themselves and losers tend to do the opposite of what winners do.

That's why this is the shortest chapter in the book. My interest in criticism is only in criticizing others. By others, I mean anyone but me. To be fair, I only criticize two kinds of people: the ones who are better than me at doing things, and the ones who are better at doing things I myself have never actually done.

Why do you suppose that is? I mean, why are winners more critical of themselves, and losers just the opposite? My guess would be envy. Losers have nothing to lose. Winners have everything to lose. That's a harsh reality for many "success seekers." It's no wonder frustration and self-loathing build up over time.

Have you ever been critical of the Olsen twins not making

the cut at the British Open? Were you critical of the Academy when they failed to nominate Brett Favre for Best Supporting Actor in *Something about Mary*? Have you ever criticized Celine Dion for not competing in the Tour de France?

Of course you haven't. And you never will because that is not what they do. There's not even an expectation those people would be any good at doing those things.

Yet losers get criticized every day for that very thing. So now, I not only get criticized for the things I do, but I get criticized for the things I don't bother doing or even try to do. Brett and Celine rarely get scolded for the things they don't attempt to do, so why aren't losers afforded the same courtesy? If you ask me, it just makes sense not to try things you already know others can do so much better than you.

In the end, criticism is simply an opinion. But the only opinion that should ever matter is the opinion of someone who thinks and believes exactly as you do. That's why if you really want to be a loser, you should only take criticism or advice from another loser. Only someone who thinks like you could possibly understand how motivationally challenging everything is, why things are like they are, and why things will never change.

As far as dishing out criticism, you should only do so under two conditions: when you know more about something than everyone else, and when it's something you have little or no experience doing. If you're already doing that, then congratulations on making tenure.

Think of criticism as a fruitcake you get at Christmas. You don't have to give it back, but you sure as heck don't have to eat it. Remember, the only time criticism is unfair and unjustified is when you're not the one who said it.

criticism affirmations

→ I am always criticized for things I've never even
   attempted to do.

→ Even though I'm not capable of doing what others do,
   I seem to recognize so clearly what it is they're always
   doing wrong.

→ Losers should only tolerate criticism from other losers.

→ If I want a job I'll never be criticized for, I should start
   a lawn-mowing service with my grandparents as my
   only clients.

→ I should only offer advice under two circumstances:
   when nobody asks me for it and when I have little or
   no experience in the matter.

→ The only time criticism is unfair and unjustified is
   when I'm not the one who said it.

chapter fourteen

discipline

I have noticed that the people who are late
are often so much jollier than the people
who have to wait for them.

—E. V. LUCAS

iscipline. It's a harsh word, isn't it? It conjures up memories of nuns wielding rulers like nightsticks. It's what my parents gave me when I was unable to stop either of the following: talking or not being still. When somebody is victorious, they say it took discipline to win. Well, if *discipline* is Latin for *luck* then yeah, I'd say they had all the discipline in the world.

Discipline also has a mystical vibe to it regarding Eastern self-defense cults like Hi Karate and hari-kari and all the others. And it's no coincidence the words *discipline* and *punishment* each have three syllables and the same number of letters, which many might argue means absolutely nothing.

If you ask me, discipline turns average lives into unhappy endings. It's not lost on athletes that the very disciplines meant to avoid fracturing bones and tearing ligaments are in the end, sadly, their cause. In fact, I believe discipline is the saddest irony of all. Think about this for a moment: when you use discipline to try to turn yourself into some sort of vice-free superhero, you're just begging to develop a tremendous amount of guilt when you do fail and hit rock bottom.

And when others discipline you, how is that any different from how we train dogs to be obedient pets?

Well, let's review what discipline has given us so far: constant manipulation, endless guilt, increased physical trauma, and a fear of nuns. Discipline is like a double-edged sword, both slowing and accelerating the inevitability of failure. But it won't stop it from happening. When you make no attempts to discipline yourself to be better, bones don't break, ligaments don't get torn, and guilt takes a permanent holiday. But more importantly, you won't have to raise your expectations just because someone else thinks it's a good idea.

Discipline is just a fancy word for control. The more you apply it to yourself, the more it will be applied to you. Think of discipline as you would the Mafia. If you don't get involved, there's really very little to fear from it.

And being "controlled," or disciplined, doesn't just stop when you graduate and leave home. Big Brother and big business have rules and regulations designed to control your every thought and move. In other countries, that's called "brainwashing." Here, we call it "advertising." Yes, advertising is a form of discipline—one of the highest, actually. Advertising turned manipulation into an art form. Its only objective is to make you buy, or buy into, whatever they're selling. Advertising tries to control the way you think, just the same as teachers and parents do.

That's essentially the core of what discipline is all about. It's about gaining power over what you're trying to perfect or eliminate.

Let me say that again. Discipline is really about correcting or minimizing what is considered flawed or weak in order to attain more power over what you want to be more in control of. Does that sound familiar? It should—it's the same method used by bullies in school to gain access to your lunch money. So when you try to become more disciplined, what you end up doing is dominating or eliminating everything you deem unnecessary, annoying, or imperfect. I'm no historian, but isn't that how Al Capone ran his criminal empire? Become that, and how are you any different from an oversized ninth grader shaking down a puny seventh grader for losing another shipment of whiskey from Canada?

Do you know what discipline is really good at doing—making you miserable. Never again will you ever be good enough, or pretty good, or good, or just okay.

In short, discipline means you are always setting yourself up for eventual failure. Not being very disciplined means your personal happiness comes before everything—including working for the man. You do what you want to do, when you want to do it—period. What you say goes—end of story.

Winners claim to be more successful because they're more disciplined, but look how they live. When they're faced with a challenge, they don't stop and think about what they can or can't do. They don't even know if something is possible before they go ahead and take a stab at it. They don't look at what others did before them and follow in their footsteps. They don't look for reasons to keep going or excuses to stop trying. They're oblivious to the reality of life's endless setbacks.

Losers, on the other hand, have a much broader, less disciplined approach. We know the virtues of patience. We know that tomorrow looks a lot better than today to start on things we've never done before. One thing's for certain—nothing's gonna get started today. Besides, if you put off a task long enough, then somebody else might wind up doing it for you.

Goals simply cannot be reached when multiple obstacles stand in the way. It's impossible. Proceeding ahead knowing there are barriers and difficulties is idiotic and foolhardy. When you have a wait-and-see attitude, you tend to waste less time and skip initial failures because more times than not, doing things you don't know how to do is just making trouble for yourself.

Winners are actually pretty reckless and oftentimes out of control. Sure, one or two might make it to the top, but very few ever do. Remember, everyone is a loser—except the winner.

Being disciplined means you'll be spending your life

doing yet another mind-numbing, never-ending routine. It's called "getting organized."

Do you know what the opposite of getting organized is? Sleeping. People who like things organized apparently don't care too much about sleeping. You can't; you've got too much stuff to organize. Well, who's giving you all these things to do? You are. In fact, the overly disciplined have come up with a clever system to make sure they get everything done. They call it a to-do list. Losers know the first thing you should always cross off a to-do list are the words *to-do*. Writing a to-do list is a way of killing your day doing a bunch of stuff you're suddenly expected to do. Isn't that why we quit living with our parents?

Writing a to-do list is like coming up with a bunch of New Year's resolutions every single day. Real New Year's resolutions get made once, and then they don't get done. That's why they're made on the last night of the year, because there's no chance you'll have enough time to do any of them. My guess is that you are still not exercising every day, you still don't own the company, and you have yet to spend Thanksgiving serving the homeless. So how on earth can you expect to reach little daily goals that are always changing?

I'll tell you who invented to-do lists—people with apparently so little to do that they have to make stuff up to keep busy. Making out a to-do list is like watching a movie on the

Lifetime channel—at some point you can't help but wonder if it's ever going to end. The next time someone suggests you could get more done in a day if you had a to-do list, tell them you already don't have time to do what you need to do without wasting time writing down all the things you know you'll never have time to do.

Here's another lie I'm sure you've been told many times: if you are disciplined, work hard, and are persistent, you'll end up wealthy and successful.

Have you ever tried to be really disciplined, worked really hard, stayed really focused, and still did not succeed? Happens every day. Why? Because there are three variables that discipline can't change or overcome.

Unchangeable Variable #1: *Luck.* Either you have it, or you are all out of it. If you have it, it doesn't matter what you do. If you don't have it, it still doesn't matter what you do. Luck is not random chance. Luck is opportunity intervening when preparation falls short. Luck is what winners are born with. Luck is probably what everyone at work has more of than you. You can talk discipline all day long, but without luck you're playing ball against a team called Destiny and the score is them way ahead, and you not having a prayer.

Unchangeable Variable #2: *Opportunity.* Of course, when I say opportunity, I mean one thing and one thing only— marrying the boss's daughter. Everybody's looking for an edge. Some believe that means MBAs and PhDs. Noble efforts, but time-consuming and expensive. Parchment may look impressive hanging on the wall, but if you're actually looking to improve your odds for success, I have a suggestion. When the boss's college-interning daughter stops by the office, ask her to fetch you some coffee and then ask her out. If she's married, don't be a coward. You'll have to ask out her older, less attractive sister. Life, my friend, is a series of trade-offs.

Unchangeable Variable #3: Obstacles. We've all got them. But some of us have more than others—a lot more. If you're not angry and bitter about having more than your fair share of obstacles, you'll not only fail to see them all, you'll fail to mention them when you need a really good excuse.

And by focusing on your obstacles, I guarantee you'll come as close to winning as if you had never tried at all.

discipline
affirmations

→ If I'm disciplined and work hard, I could end up being very wealthy—or alone and in debt. There's really no way for me to know.

→ The first thing I should always cross off my to-do list are the words *to-do*.

→ Discipline will not help me quit smoking. The only things that work are nicotine patches, prescription drugs, and eating sugary snacks when the cravings hit.

→ Next time anyone tells me that organizing my day will allow me to get more done, I will tell them my day is already so cluttered I can't get anything done as it is.

→ As far as my future goes, I'm going to develop a plan of action and stick with it until I just feel like giving up.

→ Discipline is like a double-edged sword—both slowing and accelerating the inevitability of failure.

→ Having no discipline whatsoever really means I'm insisting my immediate needs and desires come before anyone else's.

chapter fifteen

love

Love is what happens to a man and a woman
who don't know each other.

—W. SOMERSET MAUGHAM

I f you want to find true love, then what you ought to do right now is just give up looking for it. I mean it—just give up right now. You will never find it.

You won't have to because if you're a real loser, true love will find you.

In case you haven't heard, opposites attract. It doesn't matter if it's magnetic fields or electrical currents or two people in love—opposites attract. So, if you have a winning personality, chances are you're probably dating a bunch of losers. And if you're a real loser, then you've probably been calling my daughter for a date. If she says yes, don't let it go to your head. The only reason she'll go out with you is because she has all the issues that go along with being a winner. She simply can't resist a challenge.

Winners have a bad habit of accepting challenges and expecting a return from their efforts, kind of like yelling into a canyon and waiting for an echo. And if you're a winner dead set on dating losers, you already know how it feels to be heartbroken standing alone on the edge of a canyon waiting for an echo you'll never hear.

Losers don't bother with expectations, so they don't stand around wasting time listening for echoes.

But losers need love, too. So they give nothing, expect nothing, offer nothing, and always end up with the perfect opposite of that. Sounds too good to be true, doesn't it? Well that's how true love is supposed to feel.

Still, it's only half the battle. Finding love—once you know how—is the easy part. Finding someone who will remain completely devoted to you while you pursue all the things you enjoy doing is the tricky part. You want to make sure they won't start changing on you, or worse, expect you to change. Marriage is a big step, so here are a few things to consider to find out if you're doing the right thing.

First, if you only say "I do" for the money, you could wind up not working and spending the rest of your life partying. We're talking every day for the rest of your life. Not working—doing exactly what you want, when you want. Naturally, that would be totally awesome. I was just making sure you knew. Second, see if you can listen to your mate a good two to three minutes before cutting him or her off and complaining about the difficulties of your day. If she or he doesn't mind you doing that, you've got yourself a keeper. And finally, marriage has one thing that gives you the ability to see yourself and the changes you need to make to live your life more fully, more abundantly, and more productively. That thing is called a mother-in-law. And she will be a blessing in your home every day—no matter what state she lives in.

If you're already so in love, so happy, and so lucky to have found your perfect soul mate, then I'm sorry, I can't help you. But if you're a lovable loser, I mean an absolute lying, mistreating, unemployed miscreant who doesn't care about anybody but himself, don't worry about a thing. If my daughter doesn't come to your rescue, somebody else's will.

love affirmations

→ I will only marry for money. If I don't, then I will likely end up having to work for the rest of my life and never have another day of fun.

→ I will take a childlike approach to my marriage. From this moment on, I will place all blame on my spouse or on my spouse's mother.

→ The first time someone says to me I look great for my age, my days of dating twenty-somethings are over.

→ Why should I listen to my mate talking about the difficulties of her day when I'd rather spend our time together complaining about the difficulties of my day?

→ After marriage, only one thing gives me the ability to see all the changes I need to make in my life. That thing is called my mother-in-law.

→ In love, opposites attract. So when I give nothing, I will end up with the perfect opposite of that.

chapter sixteen

optimism

Things are going to get worse
before they get worse.

—LILY TOMLIN

o you know what happens after opposites attract? They struggle. Like good and evil. Fire and ice. Car dealers and integrity. Ike and Tina.

Pessimism also has an opposite. It's so insidious, so contagious that once you're exposed, you'll end up giving it to anyone who comes in contact with you. If you already have it, then you know how difficult it is to hide. And no matter how bad things really are, you'll never be rid of it. I'm talking about optimism.

Optimism is like chasing a butterfly completely naked and ending up in a briar patch. Optimism will lead you on wild goose chases down long dirt roads until you're lost and out of gas. Optimism tempts losers with promises of finding better tomorrows, reaching stars, and following rainbows. Optimism is the breeding ground of hope. Hope then encourages expectations. And once you start conjuring up a few expectations, you'll end up naked in a briar patch with an empty net.

Losers usually steer clear of the dangers of optimism. Losers are simply more realistic about outcomes and results.

Optimism is like a big Friday night party where hopes and dreams get mixed into a concoction called a "fiasco." Fiascos are fruitless, messy, and leave a bitter aftertaste. But once you've had enough of them, anything seems possible.

And then you wake up.

If optimism is the Friday night bash, then pessimism is the Saturday morning hangover. Pessimism is what you're left with after Possible and Probable split town without leaving a forwarding address. After enough Friday nights and Saturday mornings, pessimism knows that nothing ever really changes—and that is a loser's biggest asset. Pessimism may not keep you from going out on Friday night, but it will keep you from believing anything good will ever come of it.

Most losers are really just jaded optimists, weary believers, and uninspired followers. It's not because losers have lost faith; it's because losers believe too deeply. After a life full of disappointing losses and heartbreaking results, a naturally occurring change in outlook develops called *cynicism*. But cynicism is only a couple of Girl Scouts having a pillow fight. Pessimism is ladies' night mud wrestling with 2-for-1 drafts.

Pessimism is the engine room on a ship called the USS *Loser*. Pessimism inspires you to offer unsolicited advice to misguided optimists. Pessimism prevents you from trying because you always end up with nothing. Pessimism knows the truth about everything. Does being a pessimist make you a loser? No, but you can't be a loser without being a pessimist.

When you call yourself an optimist, what you're really saying is, "I'm no longer living in the real world. I'm dismissing proven facts and predictable outcomes. I'm going to make a difference. I'm going to make the impossible happen."

Here's the thing—if you believe you can really make a difference, you're either an intern at NPR or a fourth grader. And if you believe everything everybody says, you're not only the world's biggest optimist, you're the ideal blind date.

The problem with being optimistic all the time is sustaining it. How long do you think you can walk around the world and not see what everybody else sees? Sure, you can fake it for a while, but that kind of effort will eventually just drag you down. And the reason for that is a little thing called the "undeniable truth."

Well, the undeniable truth is that people lie. Displaying constant optimism lets the world know you are currently seeking liars either for business partners or for brief high-drama romances that will end in heartbreaking tragedy. Nobody seeks out and dates liars more often than good-hearted optimists. How else would death-row inmates ever find true love? Well, true love on the outside, anyway.

Optimism is good for one thing only—making sure you get blindsided by adversity. The only protection you have in the real world is pessimism. Pessimism is what it takes to snap

you out of your dreamlike state and turn "what really mat-
ters" into "what's the point?" Give pessimism enough rope,
and you'll find plenty of reasons to string up your optimism
like a piñata and beat the stuffing out of it. In the meantime,
check yourself into a self-help clinic right away. They're listed
in the yellow pages under "Happy Hour."

Happy Hour is what allows us mere mortals to exorcise the
evils of optimism. Just a few sessions a week should be enough
to permanently suppress your giddiness before somebody slaps
it out of you. Happy Hours are always full of friendly and sym-
pathetic supporters waiting to hear your testimonials of injus-
tice and end-of-the-day wisdom. You'll learn in no time how
to squash your optimism with only the slightest distraction,
the smallest inconvenience, or the tiniest amount of criticism.

But there's something even more troubling about optimism—something darker, more sinister, and far worse than
offering tidbits of hope to impossible dreamers. If you allow
optimism to go untreated for any length of time, you may end
up with an untreatable case of perseverance.

Perseverance is what turns a few nuts and bolts into
Frankenstein. Perseverance turns words of warning into
personal challenges. Personal challenges are really just expectations dressed in sheep's clothing and wandering aimlessly
down a never-ending road all alone.

Clearly, a little harmless optimism isn't so harmless when

you start mixing it with impossible hopes and improbable dreams. It is optimism that confuses brief moments of activity with accomplishments. Wasting time in those pursuits is the little-talked-about downside of optimism. Just because you're enthusiastic about cutting down a bunch of trees doesn't mean God's going to call on you to build a boat.

The idea here is not to make the unrealistic seem real or the impossible seem probable. Keep a short leash on your optimism and it won't drag you up and down the sidewalk.

What you don't wanna do is allow optimism to leave you discouraged and bitter. That's what marriage and a 9-to-5 job are for.

optimism affirmations

→ The best way I can diminish the effects of optimism is to keep reliving each disappointing loss over and over again.

→ My optimism must be keeping me looking young. When I tell people I'm optimistic about my future, they usually ask me if I'm still in the fourth grade.

→ Optimism can hurt me because it keeps me from seeing the countless obstacles that can trip me up or slow me down.

→ The worst thing about being cheery and optimistic all the time is how often I don't notice when others are being rude, selfish, and vindictive.

→ Most of the time just wiping this million-dollar smile off my face will diminish my optimism and smarten me up.

reality check

Life's ultimate answers are only known
by three people: teenagers, hairdressers,
and your mother-in-law.

chapter seventeen

wisdom

Good people are good because they've come to
wisdom through failure. We get very little
wisdom from success, you know.

—WILLIAM SAROYAN

If you've made it this far, you're probably asking yourself the one question I get asked the most: "Why can't I be lucky enough to have a relative on the board of HarperCollins so I can get my crap published?" Envy, party of one.

What you're really asking is: *"Will the day come when I wake up and find I am no longer a loser?"*

You know what? So many things would have to happen that it's really not worth worrying over. Your whole life would have to change. You'd have to stop listening to all the people you know who gladly remind you of what is possible and, more importantly, what is not possible. You'd have to be blind not to see the stumbling blocks and countless obstacles that you've learned to avoid so you wouldn't get hurt. You'd have to see what others don't, do what others won't, and believe in what others can't.

And that's just the beginning. Then you'd have to overcome real problems like physical limitations, prejudice, imperfect parenting, and envy. You'd have to be so busy pursuing crazy ideas and unreachable dreams that you'd never again have time to whine or complain. Worse yet, you'd have to start pointing a finger at yourself for the things you can't do or don't have, instead of blaming others. Then what would you do with all your resentment, anger, and bitterness? Are you just suddenly gonna change your whole outlook, stop making excuses, and overcome countless obstacles?

There are simply way too many things in this world that are unchangeable, unattainable, and not doable. Once you completely accept that, you've learned the two most important lessons in life: one, you'll know what is preventing you from winning; and two, you can justify every single failure. A life dedicated to being a loser gives you every reason to quit, every reason to shift blame, and every excuse to, uh, find an excuse.

So you see, you have very little to worry about. Too many things would have to happen before things can change for you. I just know from personal experience, and my own wisdom from being a loser for so long, that there are legitimate excuses and plenty of good reasons why you and I keep winding up on the corner of Second and Last to catch a bus to Nowheresville.

Do you know what wisdom really is? Wisdom is like a satisfying moment of understanding that you acquire only after you apply your knowledge and experience against people you don't like. But that, too, is a simple answer. Yes, wisdom comes from knowledge and experience. Knowledge is power and power is what brings you status. It's status that really allows you to avenge your enemies without being arrested or getting fired.

The human spirit is a myth. Kindness conveys weakness. Words are as good as deeds. Maybe better. Apathy, combined with wearing the right sneakers, is what makes you cool. The urge to control your own destiny is laughable. The idea of splitting from the herd and challenging long-held beliefs is unthinkable. And to even imagine the possibility of achieving something great in your life without compromising your integrity is, well, unreasonable.

You may not have started out thinking you'd be coming in second your whole life. But once you get comfortable with the idea, then you've joined a club that anyone can join and everyone can afford. And nobody—and I mean nobody—deserves to be a member of this club more than you.

It's not complicated. Expect the worst and you're not only predicting the future, you're guaranteeing your place in it. So the next time someone suggests you can do something more with your life, be honest and just say, "No—no, I can't, or I would have by now." That's really the secret to being everything you're ever going to be.

If you really want to be a successful loser in life, quit often and make excuses. Trust me, if there was an easier way to get by in life, I would have figured it out by now.

So who wants to race me for last place? If that sounds like a complete waste of time, I'm happy to race you for second.

wisdom affirmations

→ Wisdom is about acquiring all the knowledge I can and using that information against people I don't like.

→ Losing is not failing. It's joining a club that anyone can join, everyone can afford, and nobody deserves to be a member of more than I do.

→ Next time someone says they believe I can do something that would ultimately require me to overcome extreme difficulties, I'll just say, "No—no, I can't, or I would have by now."

It is not a disgrace to fail. Failing is
one of the greatest arts in the world.
—CHARLES F. KETTERING

about the author

Dave Dunseath was born in Summit, New Jersey, and spent his formative years in Kansas and Arkansas. While he managed to graduate from the University of Central Arkansas with a BBA in marketing, his love for drumming, and an underwhelming GPA, catapulted him from a life of comfort and security writing ad copy to a life of sporadic employment, free travel, and flat meats. Dave currently lives in Nashville, Tennessee, where he's been recording, teaching, and touring professionally for more than thirty years.

"Writing has an unlimited potential to bankrupt you financially and see to it you show up alone and well-oiled for family holidays. The fact that I've never received a single check in the mail for anything I've ever written proves that failure, actually, is an option. Sorry, Gene Kranz."

No, You Can't is Dave's first book. And, despite what he told his parents, it is autobiographical.